AF334185

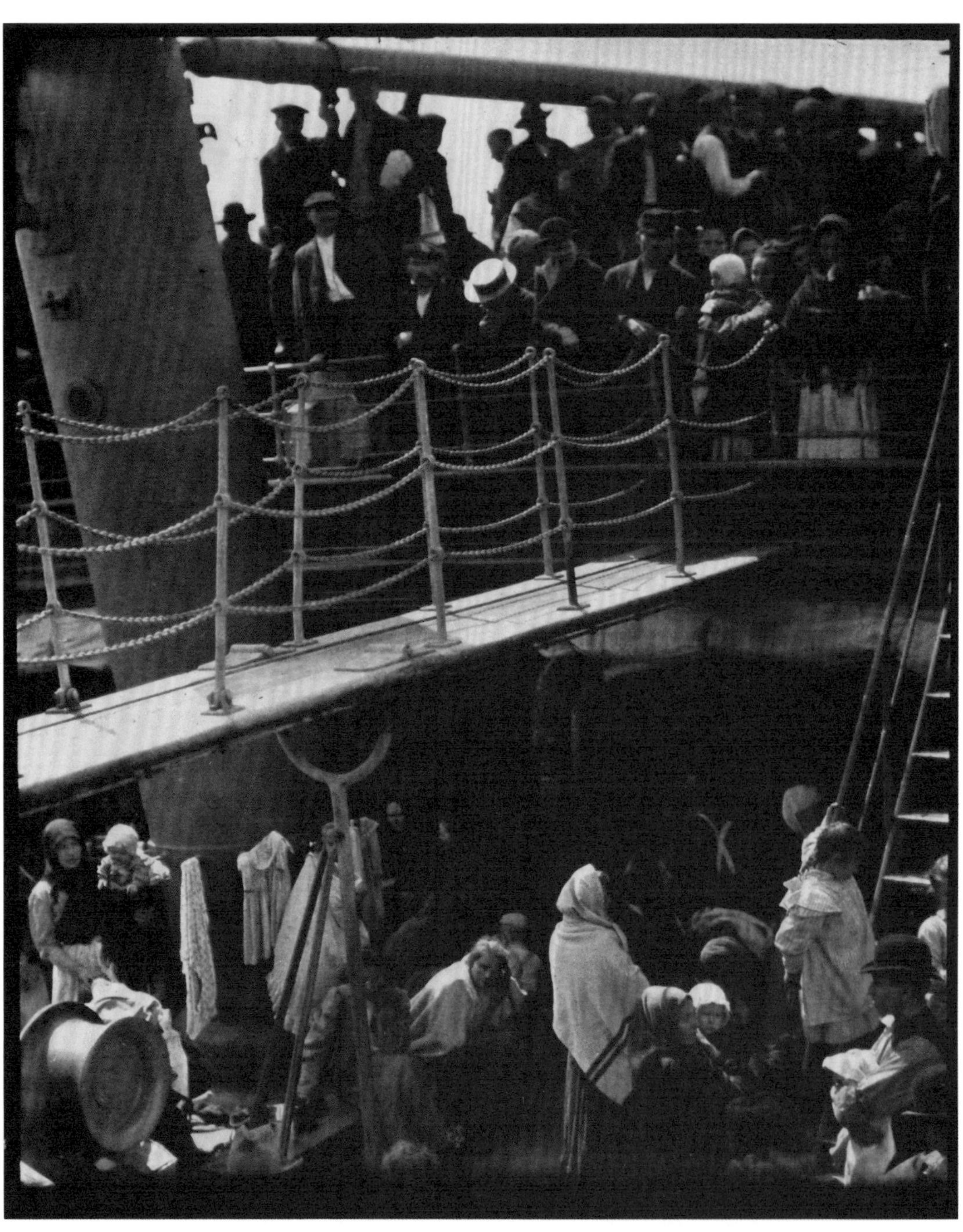

CAMERA WORK
PROCESS & IMAGE

Christian A. Peterson

The Minneapolis Institute of Arts

1985

This catalogue was published in conjunction with the exhibition *"Camera Work*: Process and Image."

The Minneapolis Institute of Arts
August 31–November 3, 1985

Seattle Art Museum
November 22, 1985–February 2, 1986

Edited by Elisabeth Sövik
Designed by Christian A. Peterson and Anne Knauff

Library of Congress Catalog Card Number 85-61317
ISBN 0-912964-26-x

This catalogue and exhibition were supported by a grant from
the National Endowment for the Arts.

Frontispiece: *The Steerage* by Alfred Stieglitz
Illustration, p. 8: Portrait of Alfred Stieglitz by Frank Eugene

Preface

THIS CATALOGUE AND THE EXHIBITION it accompanies each illuminate different aspects of the concept of originality in photographic print-making. This issue, of primary importance to all the creative graphic arts, was intentionally confronted by Alfred Stieglitz in his turn-of-the-century publication *Camera Work*.

The exhibition *"Camera Work*: Process and Image" serves as a study in connoisseurship by presenting photogravures from the magazine and photographic prints of the same images in platinum, gum bichromate, and other processes. These side-by-side comparisons reveal the inherent characteristics of the chosen media and challenge the view that the gravures often surpassed the original photographs upon which they were based. Differences in print size, surface quality, and even color are readily apparent, and it is clear that more than one possible creative interpretation lay within every negative.

In line with this thinking, the catalogue sets forth the idea that the photogravure process could be a means of original photographic print-making. Stieglitz believed he achieved this in the exquisite plates of *Camera Work*, primarily through the use of the photographers' original negatives in the printing of the gravures and through his extraordinary quality controls. Not before or since has a photographic magazine made its point so definitively.

A reexamination of Stieglitz's contributions seems timely. His own photographs were recently presented in a major retrospective exhibition at the National Gallery of Art. The photogravure process, which he helped advance, has seen a revival of interest. And it has been more than a decade since the last critical examination of *Camera Work*. Although often con-templated, such a comprehensive pairing of *Camera Work* gravures and matching images has never before been presented.

The successful production of the catalogue and exhibition depended upon the support and expertise of many individuals. While a complete list of those involved from the staff of The Minneapolis Institute of Arts appears in the rear of this publication, a few names must be highlighted. For their belief in and support of the exhibition I thank Michael Conforti and Carroll T. Hartwell. For their dedicated help and unending patience in putting together this catalogue I express my gratitude to Elisabeth Sövik and Anne Knauff. And for their diligent efforts in the many logistical aspects of the exhibition I acknowledge Mary Mancuso and Karen Duncan.

At the Seattle Art Museum, I thank Arnold Jolles, Director, Rod Slemmons, Associate Curator of Photography, and Paula Wolf, Assistant to the Registrar, for making it possible for the exhibition to be seen there.

Without the generous loans from a handful of major museum collections, this exhibition would have been impossible. The following institutions and their staff members are gratefully acknowledged: the Metropolitan Museum of Art, Colta Ives and Suzanne Boorsch; the International Museum of Photography at George Eastman House, Marianne Fulton; the Art Institute of Chicago, David Travis and Clarissa Cutler; the Museum of Modern Art, New York, Susan Kismaric; the Royal Photographic Society, Pamela G. Roberts; the Philadelphia Museum of Art, Martha Chahroudi; and Vassar College Art Gallery, Sally Mills.

Invaluable cooperation and support also came from other sources. The exhibition and catalogue were partially funded by a generous grant from the National Endowment for the Arts. David E. Schoonover, Curator of the Collection of American Literature at the Beinecke Rare Book and Manuscript Library, Yale University, kindly gave permission to quote from letters in the Alfred Stieglitz Archive. And, as always, Ann John and Adam D. Weinberg contributed to the project in special ways. To everyone who assisted me, I offer my sincere thanks.

C. A. P.

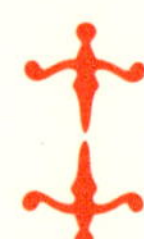

Contents

9 | *Camera Work* and Photogravure
37 | Plates
76 | Photographers Represented in *Camera Work*
77 | The Photogravure Process
79 | Selected Bibliography
81 | Exhibition Checklist

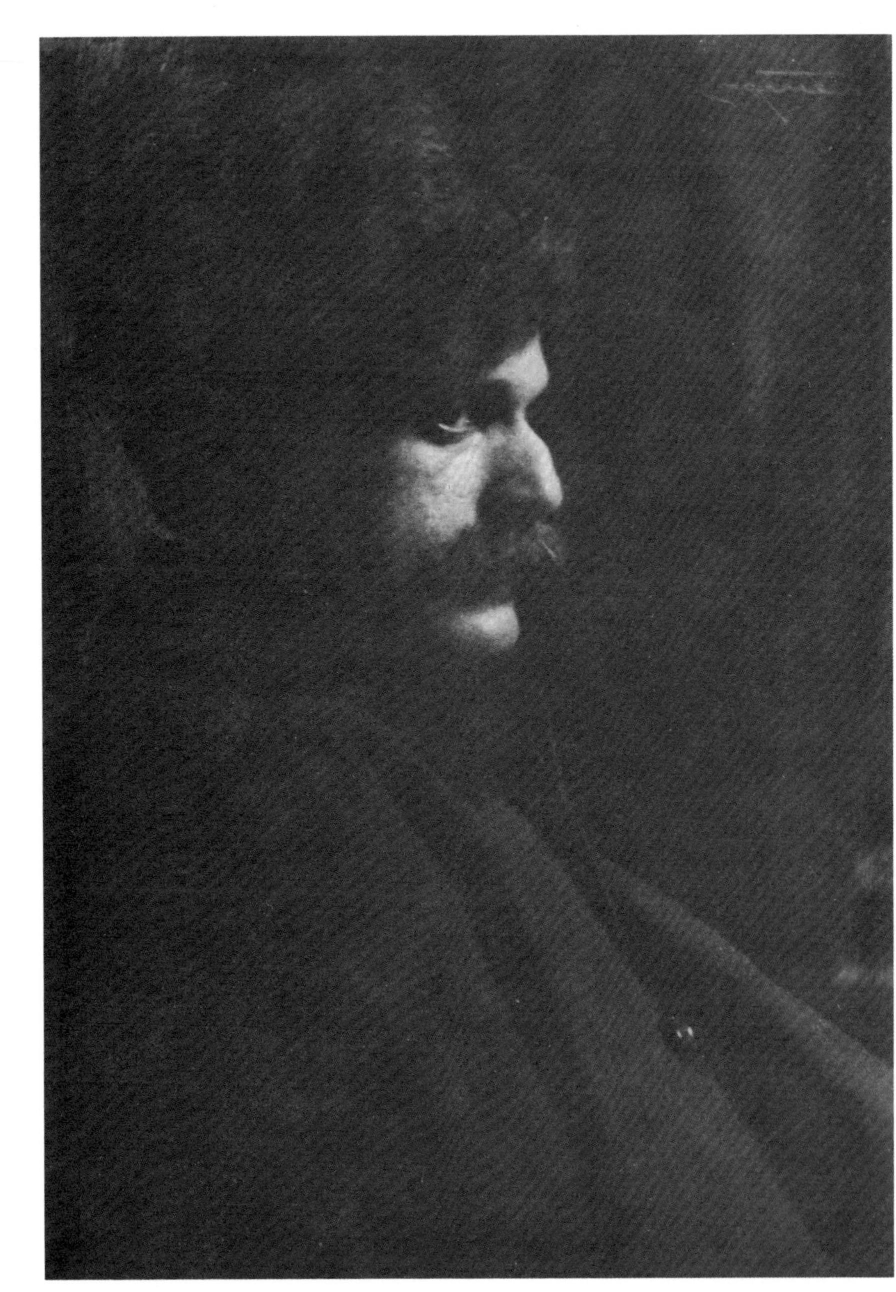

Camera Work AND PHOTOGRAVURE

VISION VS. TECHNOLOGY: IS PHOTOGRAPHY AN ART?

PHOTOGRAPHERS HAVE STRUGGLED with the mechanical limitations of photography ever since the process was invented, early in the nineteenth century. Today, most photographers would agree that "at bottom, photography is a running battle between vision and technology" in which "genius is constantly being frustrated—and tempered—by the machine."[1] No other medium accorded the status of art has been considered so inimical to the artist's aesthetic aspirations and so lacking the evidence of the artist's hand. Painters are rarely accused of being inhibited by their materials, yet it is often argued that photographers can function as creative artists only to the extent their scientifically developed tools allow: they are confined in a technological straitjacket.

The idea that in photography vision is subordinate to science formed the basis of the argument advanced at the turn of the century against accepting photography as an art. To most people at that time, photography seemed a transparent medium, presenting the bare face of nature as it appeared before the objective and indiscriminate lens of the camera. But a contingent of photographers held the opposite view, believing that the person behind the camera, not the camera itself, determined the results. Alfred Stieglitz and the pioneering magazine *Camera Work*, which he edited and published from 1903 to 1917, championed this minority stance, insisting that photography was indeed an art.

STIEGLITZ'S "CAUSE"

Proving photography an art was an important aim not only of *Camera Work* but also of the other endeavors Stieglitz undertook to further what he called his "cause." There was, first, the Photo-Secession, that loosely defined yet exclusive group of photographers whom Stieglitz gathered around himself and christened artists of the camera. This body of workers, over which Stieglitz was designated director, included most of the recognized pioneers of modern artistic photography, such as Edward Steichen, Gertrude Käsebier, and Clarence H. White. Then, there was his famous gallery "291." Begun with Steichen's help as the Little Galleries of the Photo-Secession, "291" evolved into an early showcase for avant-garde European art and modern American painting. And of course, there were Stieglitz's own photographs—images of such integrity and vision that they are generally revered as the epitome of photographic art.

THE ROLE OF *Camera Work*

Among these achievements, *Camera Work* has special importance in the study of Stieglitz's crusade for the acceptance of photography as an art. The magazine not only played a major part in this battle, it also chronicled the other efforts—the activities of the Photo-Secession, the exhibitions of

"291," and Stieglitz's own images. As a publication, *Camera Work* survives today in the physical form in which it was originally presented. We can experience it page by page, issue by issue, as did the few enlightened subscribers who secured a complete run of the magazine between the turn of the century and World War I.

The significance of *Camera Work* in establishing photography as an independent medium of artistic expression is widely acknowledged, yet certain aspects of this function remain to be studied, particularly the use of the photogravure process to present the images of the Photo-Secessionists and other photographers. While the text in *Camera Work* dealt primarily with the question of photography as an art, the exquisitely printed and mounted plates in the magazine raised the parallel issue of photogravure as a means of producing original prints, not mere reproductions.

Most of the more than five hundred illustrations contained in the fifty issues of *Camera Work* are photographic images printed by photogravure, a photomechanical process using printer's ink, which can produce results of great richness and delicacy. It has often been said that the photogravures of *Camera Work* are more impressive than the original images made by the photographer in platinum, gelatin silver, or gum bichromate. Robert Doty expressed this view in his early study of the Photo-Secession. "The reproductions . . . were usually photogravures printed on Japanese paper and tipped into the magazine by hand. They quite often surpassed the quality of the original."[2] And this opinion is echoed throughout the literature on *Camera Work*, though Estelle Jussim, for one, finds it "astonishing" and has matter-of-factly asked, "How is it possible for 'reproductions' to *exceed* 'original' prints? In what conceivable way might it be said that a reproduction could be finer than an original?"[3]

Stieglitz himself never claimed that the gravures in *Camera Work* were superior to true photographic prints. Nevertheless, it is clear that he considered most of them to rank alongside the originals as "equivalents"—a particularly appropriate term in light of his own later work.[4] The regular *Camera Work* column "Our Illustrations" often noted the difference in surface characteristics between work in photogravure and, say, platinum, but insisted that the "spirit" of an image was maintained in its gravure translation. And for Stieglitz, this inner principle of truth—a photograph's spirit—was the essence that gave life to a work. For him, technology was ultimately subordinated to vision in the photogravures of *Camera Work*.

In *Camera Work* Stieglitz created a definitive context in which photogravures gained recognition as a form distinct from, but equal to, their photographic counterparts. He achieved this task—the integration of process and image—by pursuing two goals in his editing and publishing of the magazine. First, he was devoted to quality, an ideal that he invoked in every facet of his life. With *Camera Work* he set extremely high pictorial and technical standards, accepting only images that he considered pregnant with artistic meaning and that exemplified the best of gravure printing. Complementing this dedication to quality was Stieglitz's interest in the magazine as a piece of fine bookmaking. With their elegant design, heavy paper, and fine printing, single issues functioned as complete works of art in themselves, not just containers for smaller, subordinate pieces. In the end, Stieglitz regarded *Camera Work* as "a set of important books, related to each other as volumes of an encyclopedia, and of greatest value, both monetarily and as the presentation of an 'idea,' as a set."[5]

Although Stieglitz was to push photogravure to new heights by demanding consistently high quality from the printers of *Camera Work*, he was not the first to make creative use of the photogravure process. That distinction belonged to the Englishman P. H. Emerson, the vocal exponent of naturalistic photography. In 1887 Emerson began publishing his studies of the Norfolk Broads in books and portfolios illustrated with photogravure prints. By using his original negatives and closely supervising the printing of the images, he revealed the artistic possibilities of a process that had been developed as just one more means of reproduction.

Emerson preferred the platinotype for his single images, claiming that were platinum paper ever to become unavailable he would give up photography—not a unique position among photographers. But for publishing his work he found photogravure the "only satisfactory" means. By his fifth album, *On English Lagoons*, published in 1893, Emerson was etching and printing his own gravures. Having recently learned these skills from his friend Walter L. Colls, the leading English photogravure technician, he boldly claimed that "the artist who works in photography must not rest until he has mastered photo-etching [photogravure]: then he is completely equipped, and ranks with the etcher."[6] Emerson's emulation of the etcher was so complete that he reportedly destroyed the printing plates once the editions were finished, thus ensuring the rarity of his images.

Stieglitz and Emerson never met, but they corresponded as late as 1904, when the latter replied to an apparent invitation to have his work featured in the still new *Camera Work*. Certainly to Stieglitz's surprise, Emerson gave a scathing issue-by-issue critique of the first six numbers of the journal, indicting the work of Gertrude Käsebier, Edward Steichen, Clarence H. White, Frederick H. Evans, Robert Demachy, and Alvin Langdon Coburn. He concluded: "The 'art' seems to lie in the paper used and reminds me of weak art students who cannot draw. . . . I cannot truly accept your kind offer to appear in that crowd in any capacity for as far

as I can see excepting yourself they are a lot of incompetent poseurs.''[7]
By this time, however, Emerson had ceased to exhibit and publish his
photographs anywhere, and his reputation in the photographic world was
diminishing, while Stieglitz's was on the rise.

Before Stieglitz could apply quality standards to photogravure as
Emerson had done, he needed to understand the process, and he gained
a thorough knowledge of it long before he ever conceived of *Camera Work*.
In addition to the superb examples of Emerson's gravures, Stieglitz was
familiar with other finely printed European publications. He acquired
firsthand experience in the printing business and issued some of his own
work in photogravure. And he served as editor of an important predecessor
of *Camera Work*, the journal *Camera Notes*, which also featured selected
gravure-printed plates as illustrations.

Stieglitz's first experience in commercial printing commenced in 1890,
shortly after his return to the United States from Germany, where for nine
years he had enjoyed the culturally rich life of a student. Although Alfred
had no interest in either business or printing, and no desire to make
commercial use of his photography, his father insisted that he do some-
thing practical and secured for him a major share in the Heliochrome
Company, a small printing firm. Alfred's former Berlin roommates and
future brothers-in-law Louis Schubart and Joseph Obermeyer were also
persuaded to invest, and the three new partners renamed their press the
Photochrome Engraving Company. Reportedly, they did not receive
a single order in their first year. Though disastrous for business, this period
of idle time gave Stieglitz the opportunity to carefully study photogravure
and the other processes handled by the company, as the workmen
made trial proofs and maintained the presses. He attempted to treat the
employees as collaborators, not subordinates, and exhibited his willingness to learn by referring to himself as a ''pupil'' and the workmen as
''teachers.'' As the company eventually obtained jobs and produced some
good work, including early examples in this country of color reproductions, Stieglitz gained an intimate knowledge of the technical aspects of
photogravure. Yet, his involvement in business and commercial printing
was ultimately disappointing. The company began to have labor problems
and trouble collecting its bills, and Stieglitz sensed a lack of commitment
to quality work throughout the industry, lamenting that ''speed . . . and
quantity were demanded rather than careful craftsmanship.''[8] He lost
faith in the integrity of American labor and after five years with the
Photochrome Engraving Company quit the business world for good.

Despite his disillusionment with American business practices, Stieglitz
was able to maintain his ideals and a natural feeling for quality workman-

ship. In the early 1890s, during his tenure at the Photochrome Engraving Company, he looked to European publications for examples of fine photography in gravure form, and by the end of the decade he was overseeing his own creative projects in photogravure.

Foreign periodicals and deluxe exhibition portfolios were his primary inspiration and the source of his continued faith in fine photographic printing. While the United States had no quality photography magazine until nearly the turn of the century, when Stieglitz himself began one, Europe boasted notable publications at an earlier date. Among the first was the short-lived, but impressive, British quarterly *Sun Artists*, begun in 1889 under the editorship of W. Arthur Boord and devoted to artistic photography of the time. Presenting studies of Frank Meadow Sutcliffe, Lyddell Sawyer, and others, each issue included four signed original photogravures and a lengthy essay on the photographer. The mission and format of *Sun Artists* were emulated by Stieglitz later in his own work. Many German and Austrian magazines drew his attention too, among them *Weiner Photographische Blätter*, published by the Vienna Camera Club. Its first issue alone featured seventeen carefully mounted and beautifully printed photogravures by such emerging international figures as Adolf de Meyer and Hugo Henneberg. Stieglitz, whose work was eventually also represented, acquired a complete run of the magazine's five volumes (1894–1898) and was undoubtedly impressed with the superiority of its production.

The numerous exhibition catalogues published abroad in the 1890s often took the form of deluxe portfolios rather than mere checklists. The handsome *Pictorial Photographs: A Record of the Photographic Salon*, to which Stieglitz himself regularly contributed, commemorated the annual London exhibition organized by England's leading group of creative photographers, the Linked Ring. Its photogravures were expertly produced by Walter L. Colls, P. H. Emerson's skilled printer. The most stunning such work, however, was *Première Exposition d'Art Photographique* (1894), which accompanied the first salon of the Photo-Club de Paris. Illustrated with exquisite gravures printed in subtly different tones of ink, it was issued in a limited edition available in either of two high-quality papers, with the recipient's name printed in the colophon. The exceptionally fine gravures allowed one to "vicariously experience the exhibit,"[9] and the portfolio as a whole was obviously intended as a collectible piece of fine bookmaking, qualities that Stieglitz surely appreciated.

These lavish exhibition publications provided Stieglitz with prototypes for his own photogravure portfolios. Although he had printed many of his images individually in photogravure, not until the publication of *Picturesque Bits of New York and Other Studies*, in 1898, did he issue a portfolio printed by the process. Using his original negatives, Stieglitz himself made the film positives that were used to make the printing plates, and he critically supervised the other steps in the production of the twelve hand-pulled photogravures. "We have been accustomed," wrote one reviewer, "to see the fine tones and graduations of our best workers so utterly ruined in the process of engraving and printing that we are agreeably surprised at the wonderful delicacy and transparency of these examples."[10] Considered the finest among them was the renowned hand-camera image *Winter on Fifth Avenue*, which was printed in gravure form again a number of years later, in *Camera Work*.

By the time *Picturesque Bits of New York* appeared, Stieglitz had become an active member of The Camera Club (New York), where he soon arranged for the publication of two limited-edition group portfolios in photogravure. Titled *American Pictorial Photography, Series I* and *American Pictorial Photography, Series II*, they were issued in 1899 and 1901. As editor of the portfolios, Stieglitz selected artistic work from the leading photographers in the country—Charles I. Berg, F. Holland Day, John E. Dumont, Rudolf Eickemeyer, and numerous future founders of the Photo-Secession—and imposed his high standard of printing quality. The results were striking: "The Portfolio [*Series I*], which represents a very handsome appearance, contains eighteen photogravures that are so remarkably executed as to deceive the eye into the belief that they are original platinum and carbon prints and not merely reproductions therefrom."[11] Thus, over four years before the appearance of *Camera Work*, Stieglitz had already begun his persuasive use of photogravure as a means of original printmaking, or, in his own words, as a vehicle for "the artist . . . to share his truthfulness with others." He had one more apprenticeship to serve, however, before making his stand for photogravure in the pages of *Camera Work*. This was his editorship of the journal *Camera Notes*.

Ever since his return to the United States in 1890, Stieglitz had yearned to give direction to American amateur photography. He served as an editor of the popular monthly magazine *American Amateur Photographer* for three years, but in 1897 he got his real opportunity to provide leadership. The Amateur Photographers of New York and the New York Camera Club, having just merged as The Camera Club, elected him vice president. Stieglitz proposed the publication of a quarterly journal that would not only record the club's proceedings but also incorporate quality images and provocative articles by artists and writers throughout the photographic world. The financial support Stieglitz requested of the club was modest (he expected to get most of his revenue by selling ads and nonmember subscriptions), the plan was approved, and *Camera Notes*

[14]

was soon launched with Stieglitz firmly at the helm.

Camera Notes anticipated the accomplishments of *Camera Work* in almost every respect, from the ideas discussed in its articles to the quality of its photogravures. Roger Piatt Hull, in one of the first detailed examinations of *Camera Work*, notes that Stieglitz desired continuity between the magazines and finds that "a comparison of the two reveals proof of direct lineage."[12] Of course, when *Camera Notes* first appeared, in July 1897, Stieglitz had no way of knowing that another journal would eventually take its place, but clearly this first publication was a valuable proving ground for later endeavors, both intellectual and aesthetic.

One way in which *Camera Notes* set the stage for *Camera Work* was in its attention to the important question "Is photography an art?" and to the related consideration of "straight" working methods versus manipulative ones. These topics were addressed both directly and indirectly by such critics as Sadakichi Hartmann and Charles H. Caffin in exhibition reviews, studies of individual photographers, discussions of aesthetics, and other articles. Central to the dialogue that carried through from *Camera Notes* to *Camera Work* was an attempt to define the pictorial photography movement. This international surge of photographic activity, between about 1890 and World War I, was fostered by amateurs who were self-consciously artistic in their work. Their aim was to produce "pictures" (not mere photographs) that revealed taste, refinement, and individuality, and their most accomplished efforts were published and written about in the pages of *Camera Notes* and *Camera Work*.

The other element of *Camera Notes* that foretold the splendors of *Camera Work* was the photogravure illustrations. Stieglitz resolved to show only the best images ("nothing but what is the development of an organic idea") by the very best means—photogravure.[13] The editors of the *American Amateur Photographer* correctly predicted, "Every one of its photogravures will be a work of art."[14] All the key photographers who later became founding members of the Photo-Secession had their work amply represented in *Camera Notes*: Frank Eugene, Gertrude Käsebier, Edward Steichen, Clarence H. White, and Stieglitz himself. To achieve the quality that he wanted in the magazine, Stieglitz had virtually no choice but to use photogravure, the most advanced photomechanical process of the time.

Camera Notes, as would *Camera Work*, regularly included brief notes on the illustrations, indicating the processes used and crediting the printers' efforts. Most of the photogravures in *Camera Notes* were produced by the Photochrome Engraving Company, where Stieglitz's former partner Louis Schubart undoubtedly allowed him great control over the printed results. For foreign work Stieglitz used the London printer Walter L. Colls, who

[15]

supplied outstanding photogravures by European photographers such as Hugo Henneberg and Robert Demachy. Although he had set out hoping to present but two quality photogravures per issue, the success of *Camera Notes* allowed Stieglitz to double that number within a year and a half, and he was soon publishing even more gravures in the magazine.

But praise from the photographic world outside The Camera Club began to be countered by opposition from the club's rather provincial membership, which was becoming dissatisfied with Stieglitz's worldly outlook and lofty standards. Realizing the futility of working within the structure of The Camera Club, Stieglitz began planning independent ventures. In early 1902 he organized the important National Arts Club exhibition of pictorial photography, which announced the beginnings of the Photo-Secession. At about the same time he and his future associate editors created a mock-up for another magazine, *Camera Work*. Having thus laid the groundwork for a new organization of photographers and a new publication, over both of which he would have primary control, Stieglitz resigned as editor of *Camera Notes*, staying on long enough to put out the July 1902 issue.

Within a few months his plans for *Camera Work* were announced to the world in a small, handsomely printed prospectus, dated August 25, 1902, in which he described the nature of the new publication. "This magazine will be begun as a quarterly, and will be edited and published by myself, owing allegiance only to the interests of photography. While the growth of an enterprise of such a nature must be dependent upon the support accorded it, it will nevertheless be my aim to make *Camera Work* the best and most sumptuous of photographic publications." [15] Knowing of his accomplishments with *Camera Notes*, the enlightened photographic community must have eagerly awaited this new manifestation of the Stieglitz spirit. And when the first issue, dated January 1903, appeared late in 1902, no one was disappointed.

Praise for *Camera Work* came from fellow photographers and from the photographic press at large. "Stieglitz has out-Stieglitzed Stieglitz," proclaimed R. Child Bayley, editor of the London magazine *Photography*. The West Coast pictorialist Anne W. Brigman wrote: "My dear Mr. Stieglitz, I find it hard to express my pride and pleasure in . . . *Camera Work*. It is Dignity and Beauty from cover to cover." [16] Even The Camera Club admitted the superiority of *Camera Work*, terminating its faltering *Camera Notes* after a few more months with the comment that it was "better to stop publication than to continue in any but first place." [17]

The premier issue of *Camera Work* included virtually all the elements that were to win the magazine its reputation as the seminal publication in

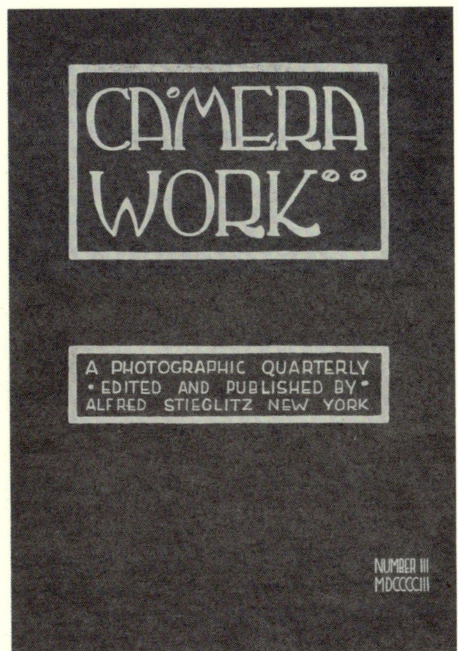

Cover of
Camera Work

the field of photographic art. There was an in-depth article on a featured photographer (an appreciation of the work of Gertrude Käsebier by art critic Charles H. Caffin); a discourse on the aesthetics of photography ("The Pursuit of the Pictorial Ideal," by associate editor Joseph T. Keiley); an examination of an aspect of the other visual arts (critic Sidney Allan [Sadakichi Hartmann] on repetition and variation in painting); an article on a technical consideration of photography (A. Radclyffe Dugmore's "Effective Lighting in Bird-Photography"); and a review of an international exhibition (photographer Will A. Cadby's notes on the London Photographic Salon).

Camera Work GRAVURES

But while all of these features contributed to the magazine's success, it was the exquisite hand-pulled photogravure plates that would immortalize the publication. As if conscious of this, Stieglitz concerned himself more with the quality of the illustrations than with any other aspect of the magazine. In the first issue, he and his associate editors, Joseph T. Keiley, Dallett Fuguet, and John Francis Strauss, stated that "reproduction of photographic work must be made with exceptional care and discretion if the spirit of the originals is to be obtained. . . . [Careful] supervision will be given to all the illustrations which will appear in each number of *Camera Work*."[18]

Turning the heavy, deckle-edged pages of the first issue, encountering one by one the open-hearted images of Gertrude Käsebier, the reader must have been awed. Printed on translucent Japan paper and tipped in by hand, the photogravures set the delicate tone that would be characteristic of the magazine throughout most of its life. Included were Käsebier's already well known *Blessed Art Thou among Women* and *The Manger*, images Stieglitz had previously presented in both *Camera Notes* and The Camera Club's portfolio *American Pictorial Photography, Series II*. He was so pleased with these new interpretations, however, that he credited the printers for their "sympathetic" efforts in producing the gravures.

The superb plates were grouped in the front of the magazine, and each was set off by a blank facing page, creating the effect of a fine portfolio. Segregated from all text, they were preceded only by a page of titles and the magazine's cover and masthead. Caffin's appreciation of Käsebier's work followed the plates, thus giving clear priority to the images. It was certainly no accident that the layout of the first issue of *Camera Work* helped elevate the photogravure illustrations to the level of fine art objects in themselves.

Along with his attention to the principles of fine bookmaking, Stieglitz's insistence upon the highest quality of printing assured the *Camera Work* gravures an important place in the annals of photographic art. But making certain that his stringent standards were maintained required his constant personal supervision. Producing the photogravures for *Camera Work* became a real labor of love for Stieglitz, and he oversaw virtually every step of the process. He made all the arrangements with the printers, getting bids and checking bills. He secured from the photographers the original negatives or prints from which the printing plates were made. He checked proofs and demanded corrections. He oversaw the printing of the editions and the spotting of the prints. And he arranged for the careful hand-mounting of the photogravures in the magazines. "He seemed to gain a feeling of satisfaction, almost of therapeutic value, from carefully inspecting each copy of a given edition, going over it as a connoisseur might treat a fine book."[19]

Publishing is usually a cooperative effort among numerous individuals, and Stieglitz did make use of his editors, especially Keiley. But, for the most part, *Camera Work* was put out by one man: Alfred Stieglitz, the editor and publisher, who at various times also served as advertising agent, proofreader, and mailing clerk. Despite his democratic ideals, Stieglitz dominated the journal just as he did the Photo-Secession group. He simply felt unable to turn important tasks over to others, and on a few occasions (numbers 8, 20, and 28), *Camera Work* was issued several weeks late because he was out of the country and could not give final approval.

An unfortunate experience with an early issue of the magazine justified Stieglitz in taking this protective stance. All of the photogravures in the first three numbers of *Camera Work* had been produced in New York under his own watchful eye at the Photochrome Engraving Company. For number 4 (October 1903), however, he allowed a London firm to print the images of Frederick H. Evans—a delegation of authority that resulted in disappointment for all.

Evans, known in England for his beautiful platinum prints of cathedral interiors, had responded with great enthusiasm to the first issue of *Camera Work* and was very pleased when Stieglitz asked him to send work for publication. He was unwilling, however, to part with his original negatives for platemaking, not wishing to risk them in a transatlantic shipment, and he suggested that his photogravures be printed at J. J. Waddington and Company, a firm he had already worked with. Stieglitz was reluctant to surrender his power of approval, but upon seeing a sample proof of Waddington's work and being assured that Evans would personally inspect and pass all the gravures, he consented. In a few months the edition was printed and Evans sent the gravures off to Stieglitz, apparently satisfied with the results, but noting the sympathy he had gained for Stieglitz's task of always getting the best out of his printers. Stieglitz recounted in *Camera Work* what happened next.

> Imagine our consternation upon the arrival of the edition to find that the work was uneven, not up to proof, and in most cases far below that standard which we had every reason to expect. It was then too late to do aught than make the best of a bad job, feeling that we have only ourselves to blame for having broken our rule. . . . For our own sakes, who have striven to make the illustrations of *Camera Work* as perfect as possible, having spared no expense or pains, we feel disappointed that this number should leave our hands and we not satisfied with it. It shall never happen again.[20]

When Evans saw a finished copy of the issue he claimed that he had never passed "such foul looking things," and J. J. Waddington and Company agreed to reprint the worst of them, *In Sure and Certain Hope*, for a later number of *Camera Work*. Still, Stieglitz felt that his personal reputation as a purveyor of quality photogravures had been damaged, and he made every effort to see that the misadventure was not repeated.

Despite the outcome of the Evans number, Stieglitz continued to insist on the use of the photographer's original negatives and the personal involvement of the photographer. These elements he considered essential to the production of original photogravures, and they greatly strengthened his case for photogravure as a form of original photographic printmaking. With the hand and mind of the photographer so intimately tied to their production, how could these photogravures be denied serious aesthetic consideration?

Most of the gravures in *Camera Work* were produced using the photographer's original negatives. This was done, just as in standard photographic printing, to ensure that as far as possible the artist's intent was expressed in the finished piece. With the negative as the starting point for a *Camera Work* gravure, the photographer's mind, rather than an existing photographic print, became the blueprint to follow. One issue of the magazine boasted: "The gravures were made directly from the original negatives, [for] the most part without any guide prints. Therefore, as in similar previous cases, we warn our readers that they should be regarded as interpretations rather than reproductions."[21] Instead of attempting to repeat the statement of a finished platinum or carbon print, these photogravures made their own aesthetic affirmations.

The photographers whose work appeared in *Camera Work* had opportunities for influencing the look of the magazine's gravures beyond merely providing their original negatives for platemaking. To prevent any misrepresentation of their creative intent, many of them took part in the editing of their images and also in the actual production of the gravures. Painter-turned-photographer Frank Eugene was given full rein in selecting and sequencing the twenty-four gravures that made up his two impressive consecutive issues of *Camera Work* in 1910. Edward Steichen almost always inspected proofs of his images and on at least one occasion hand-tinted an entire edition of gravures. J. Craig Annan, a professional printer as well as an amateur photographer, produced his photogravures from start to finish, delivering them to Stieglitz ready for mounting in the magazine. Such deep interest on the part of the photographers could only raise the already high standards of *Camera Work*.

Annan was the only photographer who provided finished printed gravures for inclusion in *Camera Work*, but there were others, in addition to Stieglitz, who gained a full working knowledge of the photogravure process. The leading Austrian pictorialist Heinrich Kuehn, a great experimenter in various photographic processes, began pulling his own gravures in 1909, the year he lost his fortune and considered becoming a commercial printer. Kuehn studied photogravure under the great printer Frederick Goetz at the F. Bruckmann Verlag in Munich, where many of the later *Camera Work* gravures, including his own, were produced. A significant portion of Kuehn's oeuvre is made up of photogravure prints, at least six of which Stieglitz himself collected.[22]

It was the young Photo-Secessionist Alvin Langdon Coburn, however, who showed the most notable involvement with photogravure. Excited by the *Camera Work* gravures J. Craig Annan made of Hill and Adamson's images and his own work, Coburn enrolled in classes at the London

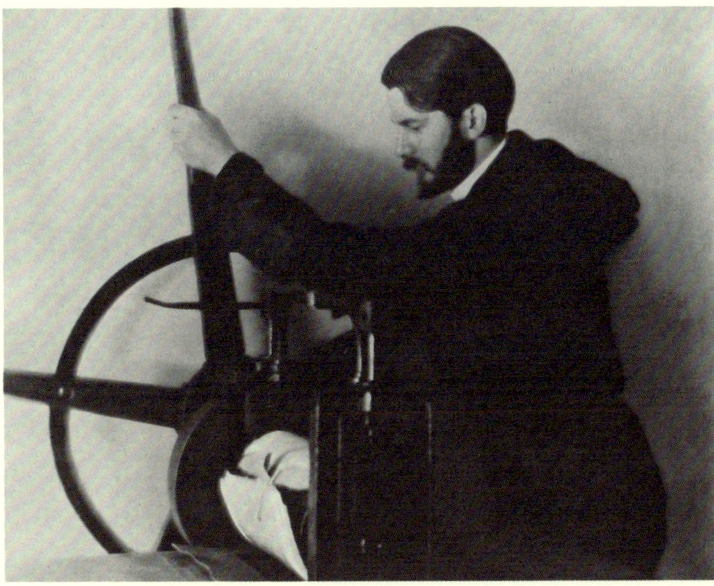

Self-portrait of
Alvin Langdon Coburn
at his press

County Council School of Photo-Engraving and by early 1909 had acquired his own handpress. During the next four years he produced the books *London*, *New York*, and *Men of Mark*, each illustrated with at least twenty hand-pulled photogravures. Coburn would prepare the plates, etch and steel-face them, grind the inks, and proof the plates until he obtained a perfect specimen for his printer, who would then produce the edition, supervised by Coburn. In his autobiography, Coburn wrote: "I may claim that in my hands photogravure produced results which can be considered as 'original prints,' and which I would not hesitate to sign. Quality of reproduction in a photograph is so *very* important."[23]

It is true that photogravure is not a "direct" process; there are three transfers of the image from the original negative to the printed gravure. Yet some of the manipulative printing processes in vogue at the turn of the century involved just as many steps as photogravure. Gum bichromate, for instance, often required the making of intermediate negatives and film positives. In fact, it seems as if some processes were lauded as "artistic" in direct proportion to their complexity. Distinctions between originals and copies, or between direct and indirect processes, were not always clearly defined during this era of creative printmaking. Weston Naef's detailed study of several of Edward Steichen's photographs has revealed some of these "originals" to be expertly reworked "copy" prints that Steichen himself made of unique experimental master prints. Characterized as "highly deceptive facsimiles,"[24] these images served much the same purpose as the photogravures in *Camera Work*.

[21]

Stieglitz and his followers viewed photogravure as an equal of the many photographic processes available to advanced workers at the turn of the century. During the course of the 1890s, creative amateurs in camera clubs throughout the world shifted their attention from lantern slides to paper prints, and photogravure, gum bichromate, and platinum were all developed or made popular at this time. Photographers usually specialized in one medium or produced negatives with a particular process in mind. Stieglitz, for example, exposed the negative for his epochal image *The Steerage* with the intention of making it into a photogravure: "In making the negative I had in mind enlarging it for *Camera Work*, also enlarging it to eleven by fourteen and making a photogravure of it."[25] Photographers recognized the unique characteristics of each process—each had its own syntax, to use William Ivins's word—and prized photogravure for its deep blacks, velvety middle tones, and transparent highlights. It was pointed out in *Camera Work* that while photogravures do not rival platinotypes in subtlety of tone, "on the other hand, the photogravure process brings out qualities which cannot be attained by the platinum."[26] Anyone who tried to claim absolute superiority of another process over photogravure, or vice versa, was simply making the classic mistake of comparing apples and oranges.

While bold claims could be made for the integrity of photogravure, such was not the case with the halftone process, the photomechanical method used to reproduce in *Camera Work* most of the photographic and non-photographic images that did not appear as photogravures. By its very nature, the halftone process, developed in the 1880s, could not rival the superb qualities of photogravure. Stieglitz used it in *Camera Work* only because its cost was about half that of photogravure, and as he took a personal financial loss with nearly every issue of the magazine, his motivation can be understood. What is puzzling, however, is that, despite his awareness of their clear inferiority, he still attempted to present these halftones in the pages of the magazine as fine prints on a par with the gravures. Among the six Hill and Adamson images in *Camera Work* number 11 (July 1905), for example, are three very flat and coarsely screened halftones that, although mounted like all the other plates, offer a sorry contrast to the rich gravures in the same issue. It is amazing that Stieglitz did not reject these prints and others like them, for he was later to indicate that he preferred to have fewer illustrations of better quality in the magazine than many of less worth, a sentiment shared by the photographer and printer J. Craig Annan, who stated, "Personally I would rather be represented by one photogravure than half-a-dozen process blocks."[27] Stieglitz's hope, certainly, was for halftone to become as refined a process as photogravure, but after 1906 the number of black-and-white photographic images reproduced as halftones in *Camera Work* greatly diminished.

Most printers had never encountered standards as high as those Stieglitz set for the photogravures in *Camera Work*. An accomplished technician, he always attempted to obtain the most out of every process. In exploring the possibilities of photogravure, he even pushed some of his printers to expand their abilities and eventually convinced them to share his preference for quality over speed. Yet, his expectations were so high that in 1910 he wrote to one of his printers, "If I wanted to be hypercritical with reproduction, good as *Camera Work* is, not a single number would have thus far been issued."[28]

Just as Stieglitz respected the work of only a few presses, very few printers could have put up with him. His high standards necessitated a close working relationship with production staff; any other arrangement would have lacked the personal attention and commitment essential to the success of *Camera Work*. Most of the *Camera Work* gravures were produced by but three firms, and in each case, Stieglitz did business with a person, not a company.

For the first two years, *Camera Work*'s photogravures were supplied almost exclusively by the Photochrome Engraving Company, the firm where Stieglitz himself had worked for five years and which had printed the photographic images in *Camera Notes*. With his brother-in-law Louis Schubart still in charge, he could be sure that his voice would be heard and heeded. As if to convince Stieglitz of their dedication, the company took out a half-page ad in the new magazine.

> The reproduction of works of art, whether photographs or paintings, has now reached a stage where it is no longer possible to be entrusted to the ordinary methods of so-called photo-engravers. Book-illustrations, bookplates, catalogues, etc., are now judged from quite a different view than formerly, when any *picture* representing the article sufficed. Now there must be displayed taste, artistic feeling, and an intimate acquaintance with the masterpieces to insure success.
>
> These latter requirements we offer our customers. The photogravure process, which is undisputably the king of all processes for reproduction of photographs, is our speciality and we were years at it before we came before the public with our product. The results of our labors in the field are clearly illustrated in this volume of *Camera Work*.[29]

This decree could well have appeared in the editorial pages of the magazine; it was a perfect summation of the editor's own attitude toward photogravure. With this shared vision, Stieglitz and the Photochrome Engraving Company produced the important early gravure portfolios of Käsebier, Steichen, White, and others in *Camera Work*.

After 1904 the Photochrome Engraving Company printed only half-tones for *Camera Work*, as their photogravure department, under Louis Schubart, had become the Manhattan Photogravure Company. Stieglitz saw this firm as a continuation of Photochrome Engraving and had Schubart concentrate on making gravures by the American contributors to *Camera Work*, right up to the last issue. Perhaps their most trying test was the issue featuring Stieglitz's own work, published in 1911. It included sixteen photogravures, among them *The Hand of Man* and *The Steerage*. Apparently satisfied with the images, Stieglitz offered the firm "a word of praise" for their efforts.

Yet by this time, Stieglitz was having greater difficulty getting good printing from American firms and was already turning to foreign printers. Next to the Photochrome Engraving Company and the Manhattan Photogravure Company, his two main suppliers of photogravures were T. and R. Annan and Sons in Glasgow and the F. Bruckmann Verlag of Munich. The long-distance relationship that Stieglitz maintained with both of these printing houses was based largely upon a commitment to quality and a feeling of respect that he shared with but a single individual at each location.

Stieglitz's contact at T. and R. Annan and Sons was J. Craig Annan, with whom he corresponded for over twenty years. Stieglitz considered Annan a "master of photogravure," a title the Scottish photographer and printer was hesitant to accept but fully deserved. Since Annan produced most of his own original photographic images in gravure, as a printer he was particularly sensitive to the process, and under his direction the Annan firm printed many outstanding photogravures for *Camera Work*.

T. and R. Annan was begun as a portrait studio in 1855 by J. Craig's father, Thomas Annan, who is perhaps best known for his early documentary photographs of the Glasgow slums (1868–1877). The firm also produced photographic copies of artwork by the carbon process. In 1883 the Annans purchased exclusive British rights to the then secret photogravure (Heliogravure) process and received instruction directly from the inventor, Karl Klič. By the time Stieglitz and Annan became acquainted in the late 1890s, T. and R. Annan and Sons had a well-established reputation for quality work in gravure.

Appropriately, the first gravures J. Craig Annan printed for *Camera Work* were his own images, which appeared in issue number 8 (October 1904). Over the next ten years, he provided Stieglitz with photogravures of work exclusively by British photographers, primarily George Davison, Hill and Adamson, and himself. On the many occasions when Annan's images were seen in *Camera Work*, it was always pointed out that the same hand had produced everything from the original negative to the printed gravure before the reader's eyes.

One of Annan's most valuable contributions was the renewed interest he fostered in the work of the calotype team of David Octavius Hill and Robert Adamson (although Adamson's creative role was not then recognized). Thomas Annan had been a friend of Hill's, and a mutual acquaintance had preserved a large number of Hill's original paper negatives (c. 1845), which J. Craig Annan first printed from in the 1890s. For *Camera Work* he borrowed the negatives again for platemaking, and printed gravures that appeared in the magazine in 1905, 1909, and 1912. Stieglitz was delighted to find a historical precedent for the creative photographs he was presenting in *Camera Work*, and he came to regard Hill as the father of pictorial portrait photography.

Annan showed a great willingness to accommodate Stieglitz. On the few occasions when an edition did not meet Stieglitz's standards, he gladly reprinted it. He made every effort to keep costs as low as possible, charging Stieglitz less than the firm's usual prices and frequently not billing him for platemaking. Annan also was very free with his printing paper. Having found a desirable Japan tissue that Stieglitz could not obtain, he happily sold portions of his stock to other printers of *Camera Work* in a gesture of true professional camaraderie.

Annan and Stieglitz enjoyed a relationship based on shared activities and goals in which their advanced use of photogravure was fundamental. Stieglitz praised Annan's printing efforts in the pages of *Camera Work*, and Annan replied in kind: "I am very proud indeed to have been occasionally associated with its production. It is already a magnificent monument."[30] Both men pioneered the use of the hand camera and chose the "straight" approach in their personal photographic work; their aesthetic stances were closely aligned. And both of them ran galleries that placed photography in the context of the other visual arts.

Stieglitz's gallery "291" is famous for exhibiting at an early date the work of modern artists like Rodin, Picasso, and Matisse. Less well known is the gallery of T. and R. Annan and Sons, in which J. Craig Annan exhibited his own photogravures and the prints of such contemporary etchers as William Strang, Muirhead Bone, and D. Y. Cameron. Many of these etchers' editions were printed by the Annan firm, and Strang became a close friend of Annan's. Along with their correspondence about gravures for *Camera Work*, Annan and Stieglitz exchanged catalogues of the exhibitions at their respective galleries. In 1919 Annan wrote Stieglitz that he was still organizing six to seven exhibitions a season and that through his efforts fine prints by Dürer, Rembrandt, Whistler, and other masters had

been placed in Glasgow collections. The exhibitions at Annan's gallery
clearly showed the connection between photography and the traditional
graphic arts. Photogravure was a bona fide printmaking process based
directly on the intaglio method of aquatint. Stieglitz and Annan saw the
spectrum of printing arts as extending from traditional engraving, etching,
and lithography to photography and on to photogravure.

DIFFICULTIES WITH FOREIGN PRINTING

Getting printing done outside the United States was a nerve-racking and
time-consuming operation because of customs regulations and the time
(approximately two weeks) required for transatlantic shipments. Production time for the *Camera Work* gravures, unspotted and unmounted, was
at bare minimum four months, and some issues of the magazine were
in preparation for years.[31] In addition to checking innumerable proofs,
Stieglitz had to make sure the printed editions arrived safely in New York,
and he acted as his own shipping agent, repeatedly giving detailed and
lengthy instructions about packing, consular invoices, and the pacing of
shipments. Though his patience was frequently tried, dealing with the
tedious paperwork and complicated procedures was clearly worth it to
Stieglitz. Without his two foreign printers, *Camera Work* would have
been a shorter-lived and decidedly less impressive publication.

F. BRUCKMANN VERLAG

On January 15, 1912, Stieglitz wrote to Frederick Goetz of the
F. Bruckmann Verlag in Munich, "I really don't know what I would do
were it not for you and Annan." Goetz was the other foreign master
printer whose dedication to quality work in photogravure enabled Stieglitz
to publish *Camera Work*. He was in charge of printing at the Bruckmann
publishing house, established in the late 1850s and by 1910 employing
about seven hundred persons in three German cities. In 1904 the company
added photogravure to the varied list of processes (including collotype,
halftone, autotype, carbon, and albumen) by which it printed quality art
reproductions for European galleries and museums. The F. Bruckmann
Verlag usually took out a full-page ad in the issues of *Camera Work* containing its photogravures, pointing out that the company's achievements, at
hand for the reader's inspection, were "second to none."

Because of geographical considerations, Stieglitz had assigned the work
of American photographers to the Manhattan Photogravure Company
and that of British photographers to T. and R. Annan and Sons, and he
had the Bruckmann company print mainly images by European photographers. During his eight-year involvement with *Camera Work*, Goetz
oversaw the production of major portfolios by Frank Eugene, Heinrich
Kuehn, Adolf de Meyer, and Edward Steichen (then living in France).
The first job he undertook for Stieglitz was the printing of color halftones
from Steichen Autochromes—a feat declared impossible by some techni-

[26]

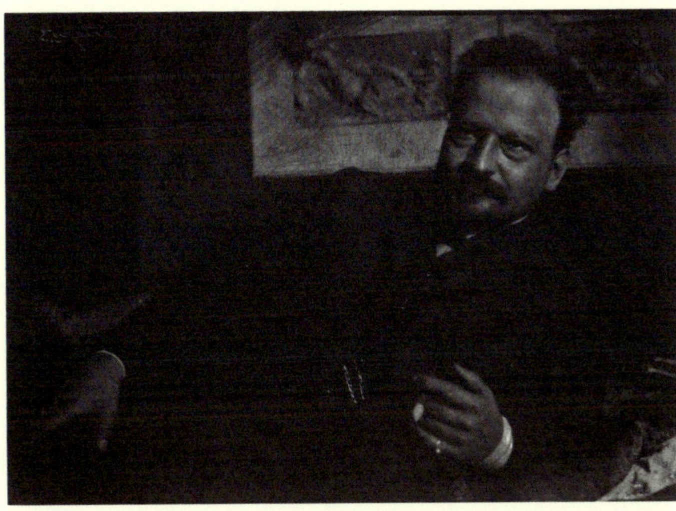

Portrait of Frederick Goetz
by Frank Eugene

cians but which Goetz accomplished admirably. It was in the process of photogravure, however, that he would fully realize his talents, guided by the critical eye of Stieglitz.

Goetz's initial venture in gravure for *Camera Work* was a tour de force of fourteen images by Frank Eugene that comprised two consecutive issues of the magazine in 1910. It was noted that Eugene's original negatives had been used for all the gravures and that, with one exception, they were printed in their original size. Photogravure was particularly appropriate for Eugene's work because many of his original prints were made on platinumized Japan tissue. Since Goetz and Eugene were old friends, the photographer was intimately involved in the production of the prints, supervising their printing and checking the editions. Perhaps in homage to this cooperative effort, a portrait of Goetz concluded the portfolio.

Goetz quickly won Stieglitz's unqualified praise and complete confidence. The improvements that Stieglitz saw in every job the Bruckmann company did for *Camera Work* prompted him to make comparisons with the "hopeless" state of affairs he found in domestic printing. Writing to Goetz about some de Meyer proofs he had just received, Stieglitz commented: "You have certainly outdone yourself this time. Your photogravures make those by the Manhattan Photogravure Company look dilettante like—what in fact they are."[32] Stieglitz developed so much faith in Goetz that he allowed him unprecedented decision-making power regarding the *Camera Work* plates. Although Stieglitz still always saw proofs, he let Goetz make judgments on processes, paper, and other important printing matters. By 1910 Stieglitz could say to Goetz, "You know me well enough by this time to know exactly what I am after."[33]

[27]

Stieglitz considered Goetz and himself kindred souls. Both were
American born, but they had met as students in Berlin in the mid-1880s.
Goetz apparently returned to the United States to work with Stieglitz at
the Photochrome Engraving Company, where he became "the sole
beneficiary of Alfred's instruction."[34] After Goetz moved permanently to
Germany, he and Stieglitz commenced a regular correspondence in which
business discussions about *Camera Work* were freely mixed with personal
affairs. Covering primarily the last half of *Camera Work*'s existence
(1910–1917), when the Bruckmann firm was printing for Stieglitz, these
nearly monthly letters—invariably signed "Your old friend" by both—
reveal the similarities in temperament and outlook of the two men.

Goetz was overworked at his Bruckmann post, just as Stieglitz pushed
himself nearly to exhaustion. To Goetz's laments about internal battles
over quality at his plant, Stieglitz replied: "I know exactly how you feel
and how hopeless the outlook must seem to you at times. The knowledge
that you have done your work conscientiously and well is really all you
have a right to expect before the millennium arrives."[35] Instead of resent-
ing the nearly unattainable standards that Stieglitz imposed upon the
Bruckmann staff, Goetz appreciated the improvements they were pressed
into making: "I can only say that the enormous demands that *Camera
Work* claim on a fellow has had not a little to do with this progress and for
that I am very thankful to you!"[36] Both men fantasized about being able
to work together on *Camera Work* in the same country. "Wouldn't that be
fine and interesting too!" wrote Goetz in 1911.[37]

It is not clear when Stieglitz resigned himself to the idea that *Camera
Work* number 49/50 (June 1917) was to be the last issue of the magazine,
but Goetz's interest in resuming publication continued until at least 1922.
Still corresponding with Stieglitz, Goetz wrote an enthusiastic letter
offering his studio, presses, and time for a final issue of the magazine:
"*Camera Work* tells your story. . . . But your life's work isn't yet complete.
The finishing stroke is missing! You *must* still make a number of *Camera
Work*—or three or four numbers—with the best work of Alfred Stieglitz.
You must wind up the whole oeuvre to show what the *master* meant!!"[38]
But Stieglitz did not take Goetz up on this generous offer, and the retired
master printer, now a professor at a Leipzig trade school, had to be content
with completing his collection of *Camera Work*. When this was done, four
years later, Goetz presented his specially bound full set to the library of the
important Kupferstich-Kabinett in Dresden, telling Stieglitz, "[Now]
your 'spirit' is safe for posterity."[39]

The care with which Goetz had his set of *Camera Work* bound and
deposited in a major art institution perfectly reflected the attitude that

Stieglitz attempted to engender toward the magazine. He wanted people to regard the publication as an example of fine bookmaking, as a work of art in itself. He desired not only to provide the best-quality photogravures as original prints but also to create a new model in the publishing field. To this end *Camera Work* was well designed, published in limited editions, and promoted as a collectible object.

The cover of *Camera Work* was designed by the young photographer-painter Edward Steichen, who had worked for a few years as a commercial printer and designer. His cover consisted of two well-proportioned rectangles, one containing the title of the magazine and the other the description "A Photographic Quarterly / Edited and Published by / Alfred Stieglitz New York." The issue number and year, in roman numerals, occupied a bottom corner. Both design and typography show the influence of the German Symbolist publication *Pan.* Printed by letterpress in a gray lighter than that of the paper covers, this design remained unchanged through all fifty issues of the quarterly.

The magazine's layout, on which Steichen and Stieglitz collaborated, comprised but three visual elements: photogravure plates, pages of text, and advertising. *Camera Work*'s simple elegance was largely due to the fact that these elements were never mixed. The photogravures, with blank facing pages, were presented in segregated sections, the text was placed between these sections, and all advertising was relegated to the unnumbered pages in the rear of the magazine.

The photogravures, with ample margins on all four sides, were carefully proportioned to fit comfortably on *Camera Work*'s 11¾-by-8¼-inch pages. All the illustrations were printed about the same size, a practice which lent them a certain presentational equality and which supported the idea that the magazine as a whole was a work of art.

The style of the text pages followed principles set forth by the influential English designer William Morris, whose Kelmscott Press produced beautifully printed handcrafted books in the 1890s. Stieglitz, like Morris, favored thick handmade paper with watermarks and deckle edges, a heavy impression of black ink (with red as a second color), ornamental initials, justified text, wide margins (increasing from gutter to head to fore to tail), inclusion of a colophon, and publication in limited editions.[40] The elegant letterpress printing of *Camera Work*'s text pages was done by the Fleming Press and, after 1908, by Rogers and Company.

Even the ads in *Camera Work* were aesthetically pleasing. Generally printed on the same heavy cream stock used in the body of the magazine, they were often designed by Stieglitz himself, and they displayed a coherence and good taste that set them apart from the clutter frequently seen in other photography magazines. Ironically, Eastman Kodak, the company Stieglitz constantly berated for their lax standards, bought the back cover of almost every issue. Proud of their contributions to *Camera Work*, the printers, binders, and paper suppliers also advertised in the magazine, often purchasing a full page together. From cover to cover *Camera Work* was an exceptionally well designed publication, one that prompted other photographic magazines to clean up their appearance.

Although *Camera Work* was not put out as a signed and numbered publication, the editions were strictly limited. At first, about one thousand copies of each issue were printed, but by the end of the magazine's life the size of the edition had diminished to under five hundred. Stieglitz was very tight with complimentary copies—his printers Annan and Goetz being among the few to receive them regularly—and he often became angry when shipments from the bindery were short. In 1916 he wrote a stern letter to the Knickerbocker Bindery about a discrepancy in the edition of number 48, the issue that first presented the photographic modernism of Paul Strand. Stieglitz pointed out that though the bindery had been sent 475 sets of gravures, he had received only 450 copies of the magazine. *"Camera Work*, as you know, is not an ordinary book. And you know how particular I am about every single number and over every single copy." Stieglitz considered the loss of even a single copy of *Camera Work* "serious business."[41]

Though Stieglitz insisted upon receiving all the issues due him, few numbers of *Camera Work* went out of print, and he was plagued for years with stacks of unsold copies. Aware of the great spiritual and monetary value of the periodical, however, he did make an effort to distribute the back issues. To ensure a "future audience" for the magazine he placed complete sets at key public institutions, such as the New York Public Library, and attempted to help some subscribers fill out their partial sets. Only after thus guaranteeing his work longevity could he bring himself to burn the remaining copies, which he did in the 1930s.

The destruction of unsold copies certainly helped make issues of *Camera Work* rare today, but even in its own time the magazine was promoted as a collectible item. Stieglitz constantly reminded subscribers that they were acquiring original works of art in the form of photogravure illustrations and that the publication as a whole was an object worthy of aesthetic contemplation. *Camera Work* appealed to bibliophiles because of the impression it made as a book, not a magazine. Many issues were essentially monographs on individual photographers and thus had a unity not approached in any other periodical. The stunning numbers on Steichen, Stieglitz, and Strand are among the most sought-after copies today. Appropriately, single numbers of *Camera Work* were often reviewed in the

[30]

book sections of other photography and art periodicals. The editor of the West Coast magazine *Camera Craft* had so conscientiously covered *Camera Work* that in 1910 he admitted, "I am afraid I have exhausted my stock of superlatives in trying to describe this handsome quarterly as each successive issue comes to hand."[42]

Cost, too, distinguished *Camera Work* as a superior publication, for it was far and away the most expensive photography periodical in the world. Annual subscriptions to most American monthlies cost between one and two dollars, while *Camera Work*, issued only four times a year, was four dollars. By 1911 the rate had doubled, to the equivalent of eighty dollars in today's currency. Collectors who wanted to make sure their copies arrived safely added a small surcharge for special packing and registered mail. As with *Camera Notes*, as soon as an issue was published, its price went up, and the charge for single back issues more accurately reflected Stieglitz's estimation of the real value of the magazine. At the beginning of *Camera Work*'s second year, a set of the first four issues, ordered from the publisher, cost eighteen dollars—more than four times the original subscription rate. By telling readers what single issues would cost them if they let their subscriptions lapse—often as much as a full year's worth of the magazine— Stieglitz helped sustain his readership and build the reputation of *Camera Work* as a valuable piece of collectible bookmaking. Such purchases as the Berlin Museum's 1913 acquisition of a complete run of *Camera Work* were noted with pride in the magazine's own pages.

Anyone who has been privileged to study an entire set of *Camera Work* knows that creative photography was not the only subject addressed in the magazine. In its later years, the journal increasingly dealt with avant-garde art and modern American painting. As Roger Piatt Hull points out: "*Camera Work* became, in fact, a digest of articles written by American art critics from 1910 through 1917. It is a telling compilation of observation, opinion, and conjecture, for it gathers over two hundred representative writings by some thirty-one critics and presents the fabric of New York art criticism of those years."[43] But the many critical articles—by such figures as Charles H. Caffin, Sadakichi Hartmann, Benjamin De Casseres, and Marius de Zayas—were not accompanied by many illustrations of the new work discussed. While topics other than photography certainly dominated the text of *Camera Work* in this period, the magazine retained its visual emphasis on photography.

From the beginning, *Camera Work* had been connected with the other arts. The Photo-Secession, for which the magazine was ostensibly the mouthpiece, had derived its name from the "Secessionist" groups of modern artists in Austria and Germany. Articles on paintings were featured as early as the first issue, putting "every other art magazine on the defense," according to Charles H. Caffin.[44] And when nonphotographic illustrations began appearing in the magazine, the editors explained that "photography, claiming to be a legitimate medium of personal pictorial expression, should take its place in open review with other mediums in order that its possibilities and limitations might be the more fairly judged."[45] Stieglitz wished photography to be considered a part of the arts, not apart from them.

Only in a few issues, however, did nonphotographic illustrations predominate; *Camera Work* presented the other arts in the context of photography as a creative medium, rather than vice versa. To soften the shock illustrations of modern art might give readers of *Camera Work*, Stieglitz published as supplements the two issues that were wholly devoted to nonphotographic work. Put out in 1912 and 1913, they included reproductions of the work of Cézanne, Matisse, Picabia, Picasso, and Van Gogh. Probably one reason nonphotographic work did not proliferate in the pages of *Camera Work* was that, for the most part, such illustrations served only as reproductions, in no way approaching the qualities of the originals. Whereas a photogravure often rivaled the original photograph, a coarse black-and-white halftone of a splendid color oil painting merely suggested the general character of the original. Such illustrations, naturally, did not enhance regard for *Camera Work* as collectible fine bookmaking. Among the few exceptions were the insightful caricature charcoal drawings of de Zayas, wonderfully interpreted in gravure, and the sensitive figure studies of Rodin, printed in color collotype.

Apparently Stieglitz did not consider *Camera Work* as much a "laboratory" as gallery "291," where he gave far more attention to avant-garde art. For the first four years, photographs dominated the gallery's walls, but from 1910 until the gallery closed in 1917, only four photography exhibitions were presented. And while virtually every photographer whose work was exhibited in the gallery had gravures in *Camera Work*, a host of other artists included in "291" exhibitions did not have their work reproduced in the magazine, among them Pamela Coleman Smith, Marsden Hartley, Toulouse-Lautrec, and Georgia O'Keeffe.

Yet even the modest quantity of modern art that Stieglitz reproduced in *Camera Work* contributed to the magazine's eventual demise. It caused readership to decline rapidly, approximately half of the subscriptions being canceled after the July 1911 issue on Rodin's work. The disapproving attitude of readers is epitomized by a letter the editor received from a Duluth man in 1915: "I confess that my patience is tried when you continue to waste perfectly good paper and ink in reproducing cubists' nightmares and

in printing cubists' talk. If those who are responsible for those productions
are friends of yours and serious in their work, you should not permit their
weakness to become known to your subscribers."[46] Although Stieglitz
knew his journal could not survive without subscribers, he refused to
abandon his "cause" for the sake of pleasing his readers, remarking,
"Circulation is fast approaching my ideal, . . . that is, to have lost all my
subscribers."[47] When the last issue of *Camera Work* (number 49/50) was
sent out in June 1917, the subscription list reportedly numbered thirty-six.

The lack of subscribers alone probably would not have stopped Stieglitz
from publishing more issues of the magazine. Anything he undertook—
the gallery, the periodical, his own photographic work—he pursued
because he believed in it, not because he had any faith in an accepting
audience. But Stieglitz simply could not afford to pay all the production
costs of *Camera Work* by himself. When he began publishing the magazine
in 1903, he had nearly 650 subscribers, and with the premium single-issue
prices he charged, he may have approached breaking even on a few
numbers. A steady decrease in subscribers after about 1910, however,
caused financial problems that clearly contributed to the demise of the
magazine in 1917.

After the June 1913 special number, the eight remaining issues of
Camera Work came out only sporadically, not keeping to the prescribed
quarterly schedule. This irregularity only added to the irritation of subscribers, who now became confused by the journal's continued existence.
But other activities had begun to capture Stieglitz's interest at the expense
of *Camera Work*. Gallery "291" continued to be an active exhibition space
demanding day-to-day attention, and the role of consultant for the
landmark 1913 Armory Show of modern art required much time. Stieglitz
even allowed himself to become involved in yet another publication,
the short-lived proto-Dada *291*, as well as in de Zayas's Modern Gallery, a
commercial incarnation of the "291" gallery. With the beginning of
World War I in Europe in 1913, obtaining the quality printing that he was
accustomed to from his German firm became increasingly difficult, and
Camera Work appeared only when Stieglitz found outstanding material
worthy of the great effort of putting out the magazine.

As early as 1912 Stieglitz had forseen the inevitable end of *Camera Work*.
"I wonder how many more [issues] there will be," he wrote Frank Eugene.
"You know that as soon as I feel there is nothing more to add to the real
value of the publication I shall quit."[48] As a consequence of this attitude,
many of the last issues of *Camera Work* have a summary air and a strongly
self-contained appearance. First there was the special number of June
1913, which with reproductions of work by Cézanne and Picasso and an

article by Gertrude Stein commemorated Stieglitz's role in the development of modern art. Next came Edward Steichen's double number—a wide selection of his work, including paintings—which was his last showing in *Camera Work*. Particularly backward-looking was issue number 47, with over sixty answers to the question "What is '291'?" most of them praising the achievements of the gallery.

Although any of these issues would have made a fitting finale, *Camera Work* number 49/50 (June 1917) was the last one published. It presented the uncompromisingly straight photographs of Paul Strand. The photogravures, made with Strand's original negatives, were printed on a paper heavier and stiffer than the customary Japan tissue, to emphasize the "brutal directness" of the images.[49] Strand's work foretold the development of a truly modern aesthetic of photography, which in its pursuit of pure form and abstraction would leave the sentimentality of pictorialism far behind.

The termination of *Camera Work* was not a defeat for Stieglitz; it was a victory. In his fourteen-year editorship of *Camera Work*, Stieglitz had used photogravure to put photography on an equal footing with the other arts. His unrelenting demands for perfection from his printers and his unflagging dedication to quality in every aspect of the publication resulted in striking accomplishments. Machinery and technology were made to serve the artist's vision, and photogravure, a process generally considered merely reproductive, achieved the status of an artistic medium.

> Undoubtedly the chief features of *Camera Work* have been the manner of presentation of the pictures and the quality of the reproductions. In many instances these "reproductions" can in reality be considered original prints, having been made directly from the original negatives and printed in the spirit of the original picture and retaining all its quality.[50]

The evocative photogravures of *Camera Work* not only preserved the originals, they became the originals.

NOTES

1. William Crawford, *The Keepers of Light: A History and Working Guide to Early Photographic Processes*, Morgan and Morgan, Dobbs Ferry, N.Y., 1979, p. 6.
2. Robert Doty, *Photo-Secession: Photography as a Fine Art*, George Eastman House, Rochester, N.Y., 1960, p. 33.
3. Estelle Jussim, "Technology or Aesthetics: Alfred Stieglitz and Photogravure," *History of Photography*, January 1979 (vol. 3, no. 1), p. 81.
4. In 1922 Stieglitz began an ongoing and evocative series of cloud photographs reflecting his emotional states, which he called *Equivalents.*
5. Roger Piatt Hull, *"Camera Work": An American Quarterly*, Ph.D. dissertation, Northwestern University, 1970, p. 55. (University Microfilms International, Ann Arbor, Mich.)
6. P. H. Emerson, *Wild Life on a Tidal Water*, Sampson Low and Company, London, 1890, preface.
7. P. H. Emerson to Alfred Stieglitz, 1904. Quoted in Nancy Newhall, *P. H. Emerson: The Fight for Photography as a Fine Art*, Aperture, Millerton, N.Y., 1975, p. 119.
8. Alfred Stieglitz, quoted in Dorothy Norman, *Alfred Stieglitz: An American Seer*, Random House, New York, 1973, p. 35.
9. Weston J. Naef, *The Collection of Alfred Stieglitz: Fifty Pioneers of Modern Photography*, Metropolitan Museum of Art and Viking Press, New York, 1978, p. 30.
10. William M. Murray, review of *Picturesque Bits of New York and Other Studies*, in *Camera Notes*, January 1898 (vol. 1, no. 3), p. 84.
11. Joseph T. Keiley, "The Portfolio," review of *American Pictorial Photography, Series I*, in *Camera Notes*, October 1899 (vol. 3, no. 2), p. 86.
12. Hull, *"Camera Work,"* p. 9.
13. *Camera Notes*, July 1897 (vol. 1, no. 1), p. 3.
14. Our Table, *American Amateur Photographer*, July 1897 (vol. 9, no. 7), p. 337.
15. Alfred Stieglitz, *Camera Work* prospectus, dated August 25, 1902, Alfred Stieglitz Archive, Collection of American Literature, Beinecke Rare Book and Manuscript Library, Yale University, New Haven, Conn.
16. Anne W. Brigman to Alfred Stieglitz, January 9, 1903, Beinecke.
17. Juan C. Abel, "Last Word," *Camera Notes*, [1903] (vol. 6, no. 4), p. 179.
18. Alfred Stieglitz, Joseph T. Keiley, Dallett Fuguet, and John Francis Strauss, "An Apology," *Camera Work*, no. 1 (January 1903), p. 15.
19. Hull, *"Camera Work,"* p. 52.
20. Our Illustrations, *Camera Work*, no. 4 (October 1903), p. 25.
21. Our Plates, *Camera Work*, no. 29 (January 1910), p. 61.
22. See Naef, *The Collection of Alfred Stieglitz*, pp. 402–409.
23. *Alvin Langdon Coburn, Photographer: An Autobiography*, edited by Helmut and Alison Gernsheim, Frederick A. Praeger, New York, 1966, p. 76.
24. Naef, *The Collection of Alfred Stieglitz*, p. 443.
25. Alfred Stieglitz, "Four Happenings: III. How *The Steerage* Happened," *Twice a Year*, Fall/Winter 1942 (no. 8/9), p. 130.
26. Our Illustrations, *Camera Work*, no. 38 (April 1912), p. 22.
27. J. Craig Annan to Alfred Stieglitz, June 22, 1904, Beinecke.
28. Alfred Stieglitz to Frederick Goetz, October 11, 1910, Beinecke.
29. *Camera Work*, no. 1 (January 1903), n. pag.
30. J. Craig Annan to Alfred Stieglitz, December 13, 1903, Beinecke.
31. For instance, issue no. 42/43 (April/July 1913) stated, "This Number of *Camera Work* has been in hand for several years."

32. Alfred Stieglitz to Frederick Goetz, December 20, 1911, Beinecke.
33. Alfred Stieglitz to Frederick Goetz, May 27, 1910, Beinecke.
34. Sue Davidson Lowe, *Stieglitz: A Memoir/Biography*, Farrar, Straus and Giroux, New York, 1983, p. 166.
35. Alfred Stieglitz to Frederick Goetz, September 14, 1912, Beinecke.
36. Frederick Goetz to Alfred Stieglitz, September 9, 1910, Beinecke.
37. Frederick Goetz to Alfred Stieglitz, January 9, 1911, Beinecke.
38. Frederick Goetz to Alfred Stieglitz, October 31, 1922, Beinecke.
39. Frederick Goetz to Alfred Stieglitz, September 4, 1926, Beinecke.
40. Susan Otis Thompson describes Morris's work in *American Book Design and William Morris*, R. R. Bowker Company, New York, 1977, pp. 25–26.
41. Alfred Stieglitz to the Knickerbocker Bindery, November 9, 1916, Beinecke.
42. [Fayette J. Clute], review of *Camera Work*, no. 30, in *Camera Craft*, June 1910 (vol. 17, no. 6), p. 251.
43. Hull, *"Camera Work,"* p. 24.
44. Charles H. Caffin to Alfred Stieglitz, December 17, 1903, Beinecke.
45. Our Illustrations, *Camera Work*, no. 32 (October 1910), p. 47.
46. L. B. Manley to Alfred Stieglitz, January 11, 1915, Beinecke.
47. Alfred Stieglitz to Benjamin De Casseres, January 21, 1915, Beinecke.
48. Alfred Stieglitz to Frank Eugene, October 28, 1912, Beinecke.
49. Our Illustrations, *Camera Work*, no. 49/50 (June 1917), p. 36.
50. "Camera Work, 1906: An Announcement," *Camera Work*, no. 12 (October 1905), front insert.

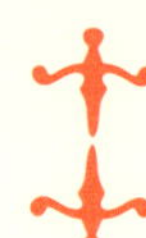

Plates

J. Craig Annan
Scottish, 1864–1946
The Etching Printer—William Strang, Esq., A.R.A.
1902
Camera Work, no. 19 (July 1907)

J. Craig Annan was unique among contributors to *Camera Work*, for not only was he an accomplished photographer, but he also served as the printer for many of the photogravures in the periodical. This expressive portrait of his close friend William Strang (1859–1921) was undoubtedly made at the firm of T. and R. Annan and Sons, where Annan oversaw the printing of etchings and engravings by such contemporary printmakers as Muirhead Bone, D. Y. Cameron, and Strang. It shows the artist effectively framed by manipulated open space and the tools of the trade. In the issue that carried the portrait, the editors of *Camera Work* wrote, "As the gravure plates and the edition therefrom have virtually been made by Mr. Annan himself, this series [of five images] has an increased interest and value, for their quality as gravures is as remarkable as the quality of the original prints." In addition to printing his own photogravures for *Camera Work*, Annan produced gravures of work by the British photographers George Davison and Hill and Adamson.

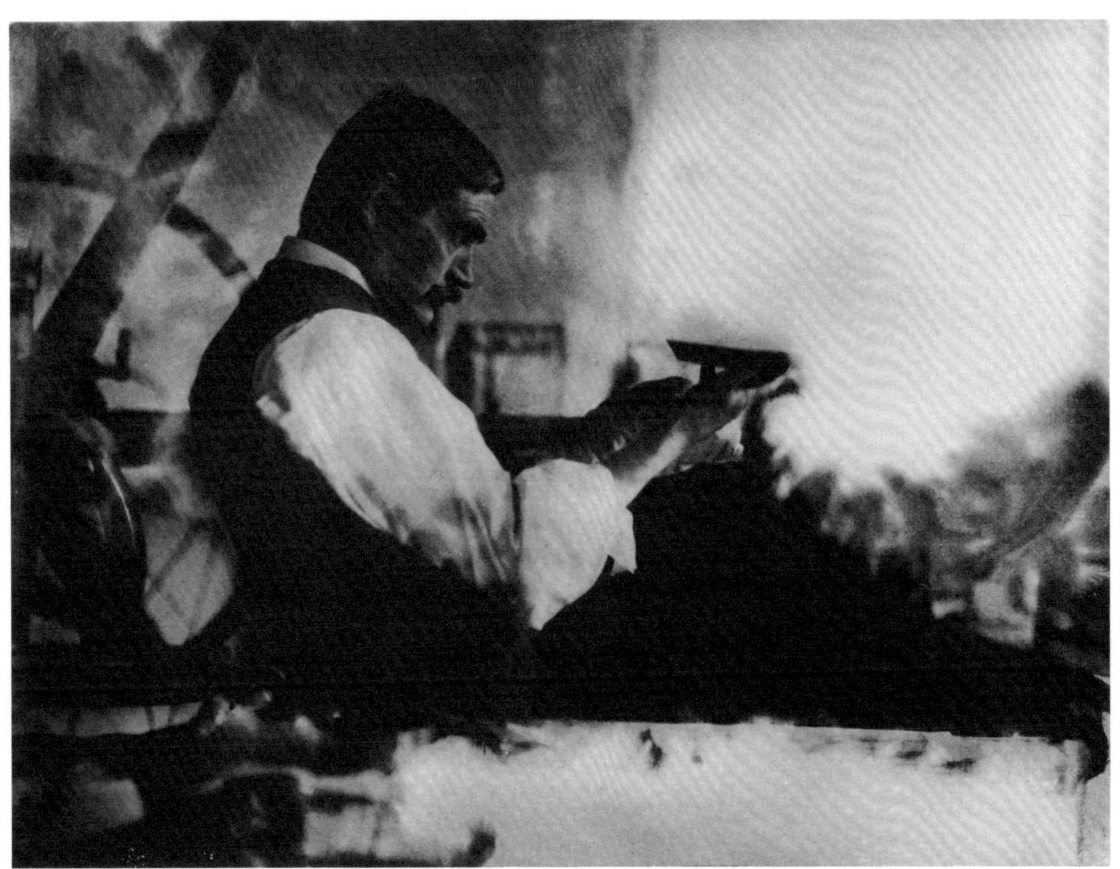

American, 1869–1950
The Source
c. 1906
Camera Work, no. 25 (January 1909)

Anne W. Brigman was one of the few photographers from the West Coast to become a member of the Photo-Secession group and have her images appear in *Camera Work*. Making only one trip to New York—in 1910, when she met Stieglitz, whom she idolized—Brigman remained isolated from the center of pictorial activity, and she expressed an exotic freedom in images that often intertwined female nudes with barren coastal rocks and trees. Unlike most of her contemporaries, who worked mainly in platinum or gum bichromate, she made primarily bromide (gelatin silver) enlargements from small negatives, many of which, unfortunately, exhibit rather unrefined handwork. Her well-known allegory *The Source*, however, is one of her most successful images—a peaceful, archetypal scene cleanly and confidently printed. Later in life Brigman turned to poetry, producing in 1949 the book *Song of a Pagan*, which combined her writing with her photographs.

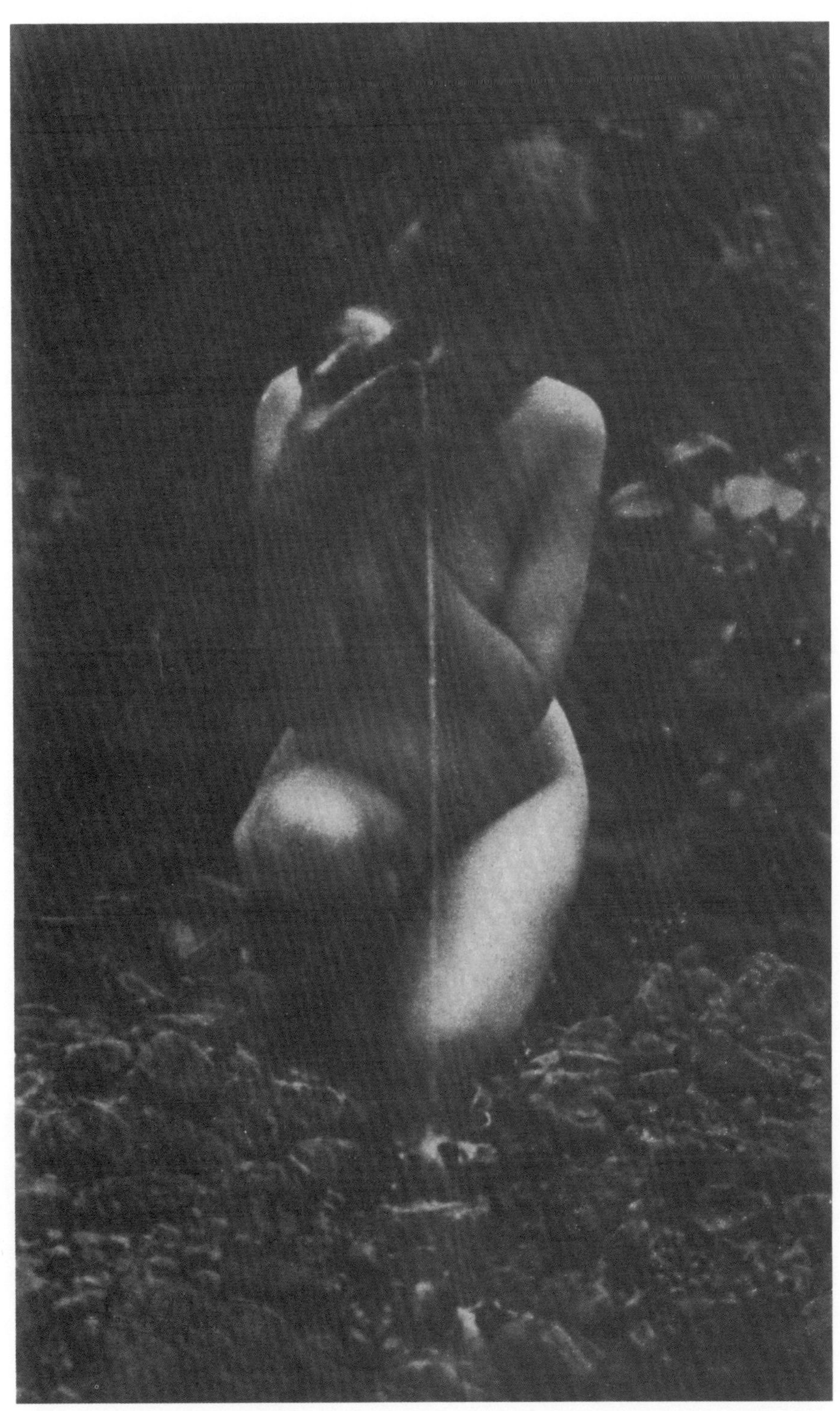

JULIA MARGARET CAMERON
English (b. India), 1815–1879
Carlyle
1867
Camera Work, no. 41 (January 1913)

Now regarded as one of the great masters of portrait photography, Julia Margaret Cameron was little known at the turn of the century. Stieglitz apparently first learned of her from Joseph T. Keiley, who came across her work while visiting England in 1908. The Autotype Fine Arts Company, a London publishing house, held some of Cameron's original 10-by-12-inch negatives and made the plates used to print the five photogravures of her work that appeared in *Camera Work*. Cameron aggressively photographed numerous eminent Victorians who were her friends, among them the historian and essayist Thomas Carlyle (1795–1881). With her characteristic disregard for technique, Cameron here produced an image greatly out of focus; yet the portrait resonates with insight, energy, and spontaneity. Stieglitz promoted Cameron, along with the Scottish team of Hill and Adamson, as a pioneer of pictorial photography.

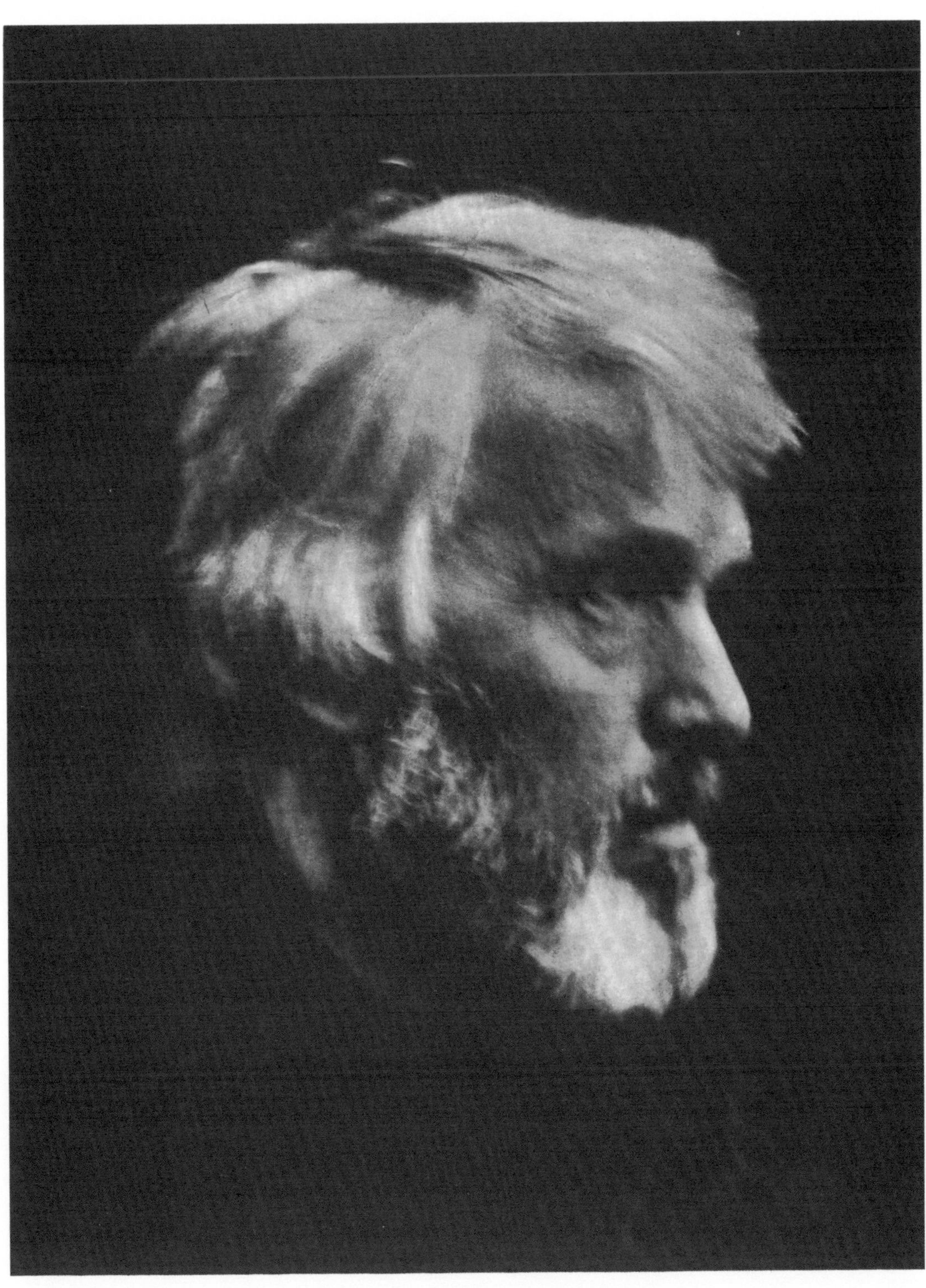

ALVIN LANGDON COBURN
English (b. United States), 1882–1966
The Bridge—London
c. 1903
Camera Work, no. 15 (July 1906)

Having begun to photograph at an early age, Alvin Langdon Coburn
became the youngest major member of the Photo-Secession. He studied
with some of the older pictorialists, like his distant cousin F. Holland Day
and Gertrude Käsebier, but soon established a reputation for his pioneering
and skillful use of gum-platinum printing. This process, a combination of
the platinum and gum-bichromate methods, involves coating platinotypes
with gum solutions. Gum-platinum prints of *The Bridge—London* exhibit
all the strengths of the process: a clean underlying image with smooth
middle values; rich shadow areas that suggest great depth; and a surface in
slight relief with a pleasant, lustrous patina. In about 1909 Coburn settled
permanently in England and began to concentrate on another creative
printmaking process—photogravure. He produced a number of fine books
with hand-pulled gravures from his own press, the first of which (*London*,
1909) included a print of *The Bridge—London*.

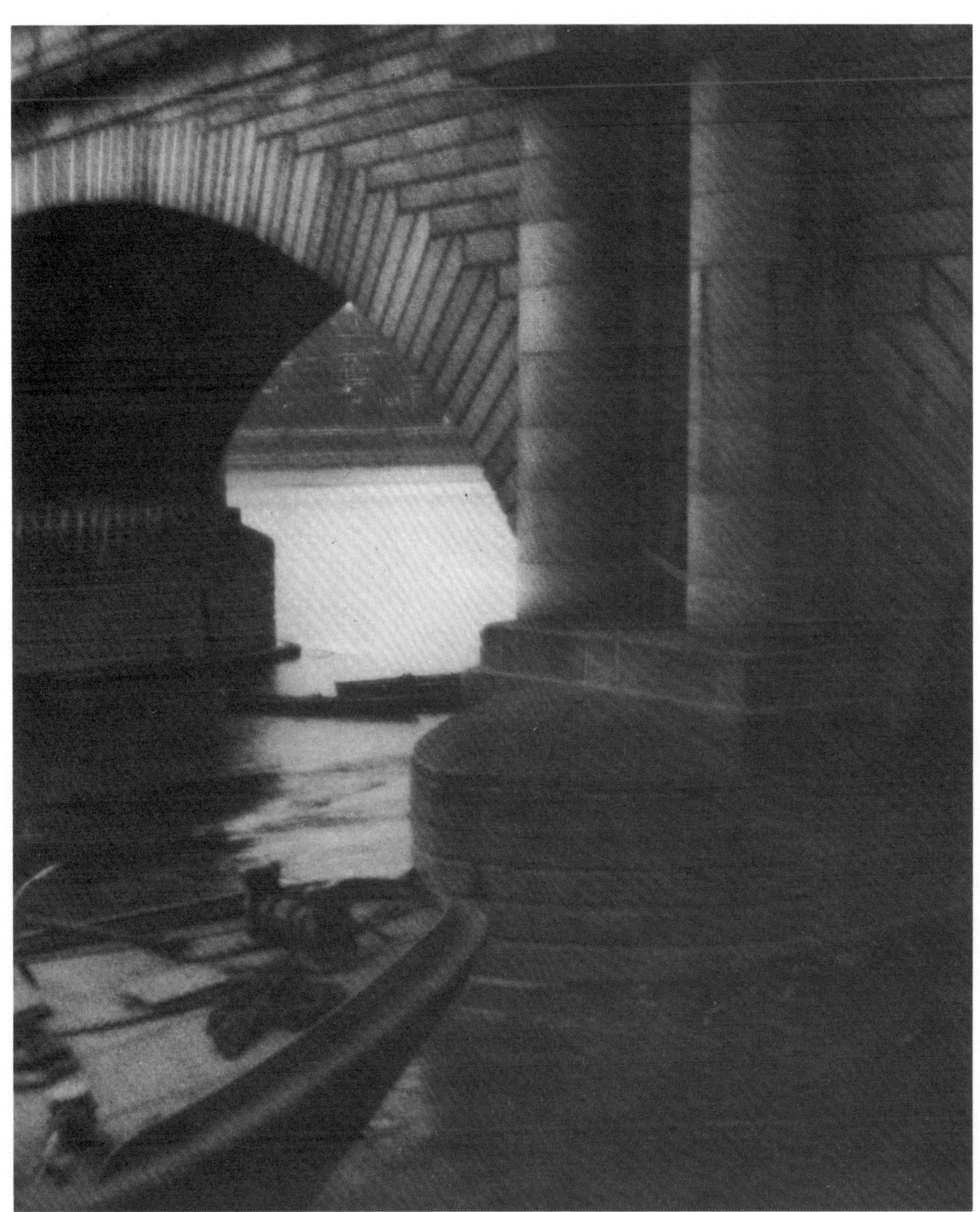

Robert Demachy
French, 1859–1936
Toucques Valley
1902
Camera Work, no. 16 (October 1906)

The leading French pictorialist at the turn of the century, Robert Demachy was an accomplished manipulative printmaker, a prolific writer, and a founding member of the Photo-Club de Paris, the French counterpart of America's Photo-Secession and Britain's Linked Ring. In countless articles and many books, he advocated the use of the gum-bichromate and oil processes, both of which allowed extensive hand manipulation of the image and of the print's surface. His early gum prints generated widespread interest in the medium and even attracted attention from Stieglitz, a consummate purist. Many of them show the painterly effects possible in gum, and his deep-toned photogravure *Toucques Valley* resembles a Barbizon school charcoal drawing. Inexplicably, Demachy gave up photography at the beginning of World War I.

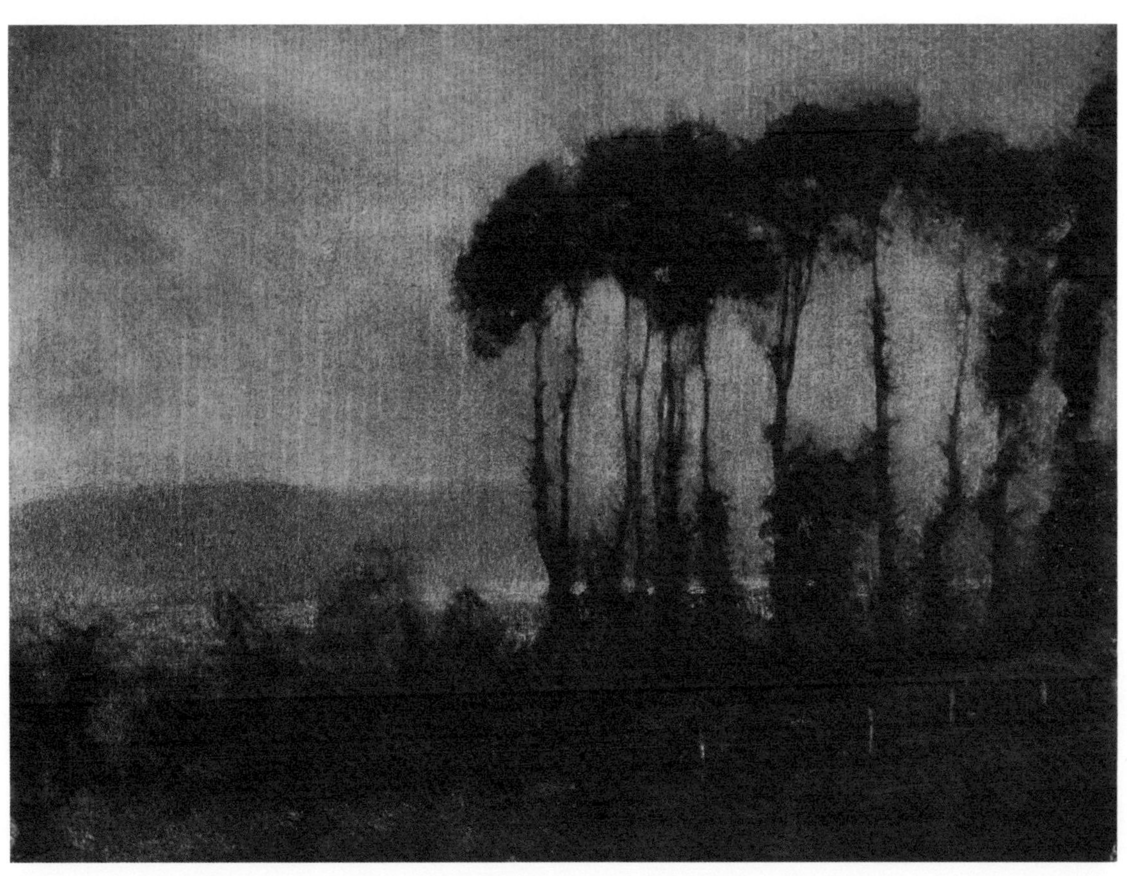

Residing variously in Dresden, London, Paris, and New York, and affecting numerous other names for himself, Baron Adolf de Meyer led the life of a cosmopolitan aristocrat and aesthete. The style of his photographic still lifes and portraits of notable personalities was refined and self-conscious, as is evident in this image, with its radically unbalanced composition and soft middle values. Writing in the January 1912 issue of *Camera Work* on a related piece, the art critic Charles H. Caffin characterized the mood of this photograph as well: "In its purity of color, the magic of its shimmering light and evanescent half-tones, and the *enveloppe* of silky atmosphere which unites everything into an ensemble of impression, it is a veritable dream of loveliness. The poetry, latent in the material, hovers like fragrant breath over the whole conception." By the time *Camera Work* ceased publication in 1917, de Meyer had begun to transform fashion photography into an art form through his innovative work for Condé Nast's *Vogue*.

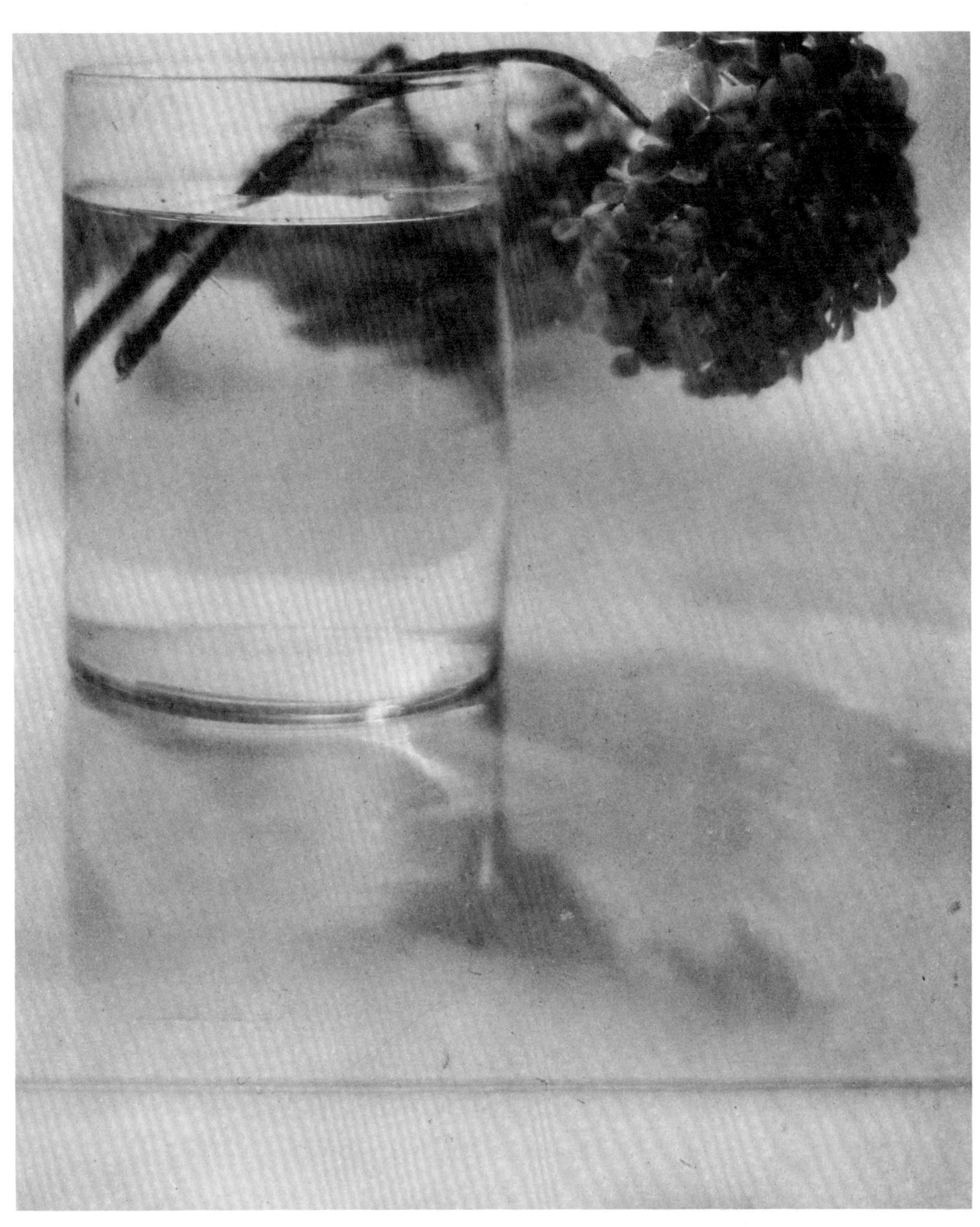

American, 1860–1931
L'Allegro
1902
Camera Work, no. 18 (April 1907)

Little is known about William B. Dyer, a founding member of Stieglitz's
Photo-Secession group who is represented in *Camera Work* by only two
photogravures. He apparently lived in Chicago during the first decade of
the century and then moved west. In addition to pursuing creative photography, Dyer worked as a commercial photographer specializing in book
illustration, James Whitcomb Riley's *Love Lyrics* being his best-known
effort. *L'Allegro* may have been intended as an illustration for a poem of
the same title by the seventeenth-century English poet John Milton.
The photograph presents a stylized nude against a stark background,
prefiguring similar friezelike work by William Mortensen and Arthur F.
Kales. Dyer reportedly was one of the few Americans to enthusiastically
adopt the gum-bichromate process, but only a handful of his original
prints have survived.

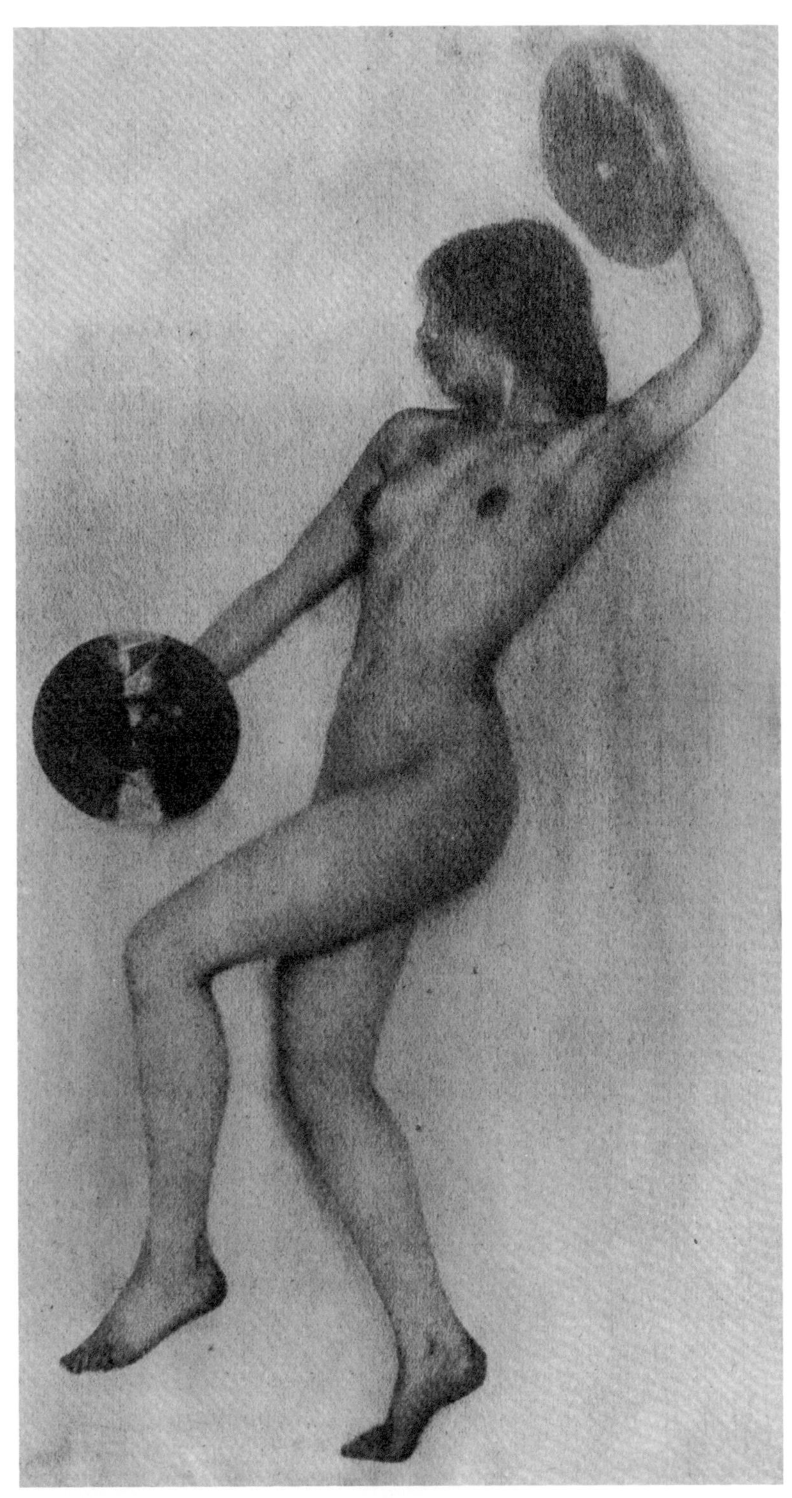

German (b. United States), 1865–1936
Lady of Charlotte
c. 1899
Camera Work, no. 25 (January 1909)

Frank Eugene (born Frank Eugene Smith), a recognized painter of
Jugendstil-like canvases, was one of the best-represented photographers in
Camera Work. In 1906 he established permanent residence in Germany,
where he became associated with such artists as Fritz von Uhde, Willy
Geiger, and Franz von Stuck. He soon was concentrating on photographic
work, however, and in 1913 was appointed to the world's first chair in
pictorial photography, at the Royal Academy of Graphic Arts in Leipzig.
A skilled etcher, Eugene marked and scratched many of his negatives to
achieve the expressiveness he desired. *Lady of Charlotte*, which shows
Eugene's characteristic handwork, was apparently one of Stieglitz's
favorite images. Photogravures of it appeared not only in *Camera Work*,
but also in *Camera Notes* (April 1900) and in the portfolio *American Pictorial
Photography, Series II* (1901), both edited by Stieglitz. The sinuous lines of
the image, and the figure's suggestive pose, clearly reflect Art Nouveau and
Symbolist influences.

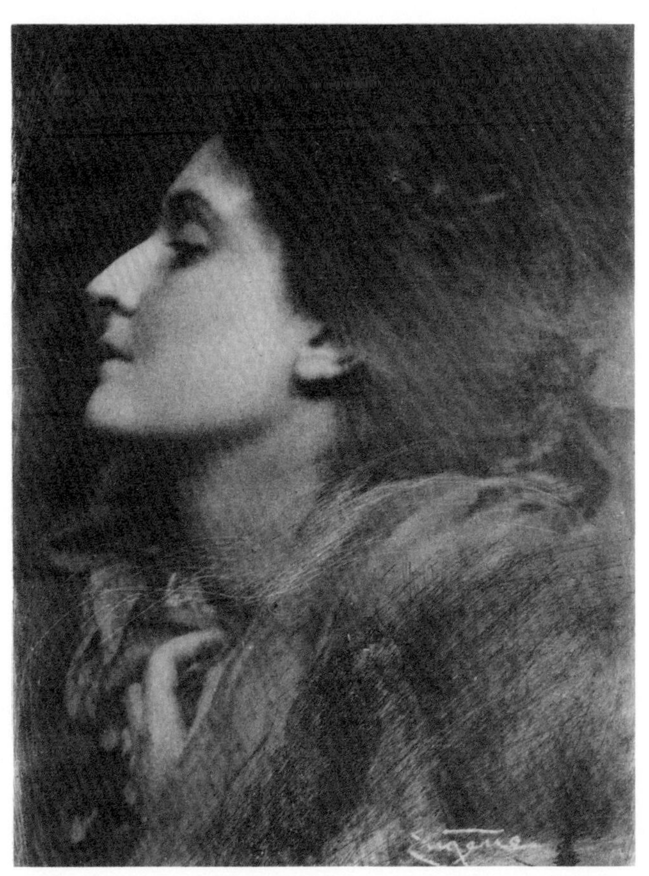

FREDERICK H. EVANS
English, 1853–1943
Ely Cathedral: Across Nave and Octagon
1903
Camera Work, no. 4 (October 1903)

Frederick H. Evans ran a small bookshop in London until 1898, when he retired and devoted himself to photography and family life. He is renowned for his photographs of cathedral interiors. Always printed on platinum paper, in the straightest of styles, they capture the light and volume of architectural structures that Evans considered islands of calm and dignity in the busy world. *Ely Cathedral* is a prime example of his skill at portraying spatial relationships. Evans paid careful attention to the mounting of his delicate prints, often backing them with multiple layers of subtly colored paper or framing them in hand-ruled linear borders. When platinum paper became commercially unavailable in the 1920s, Evans gave up printing from his negatives. Although his work appeared in but a single, early issue of *Camera Work*, he continued to follow the publication as late as 1915, when, owing to poverty, he traded original prints to Stieglitz for certain numbers of the magazine.

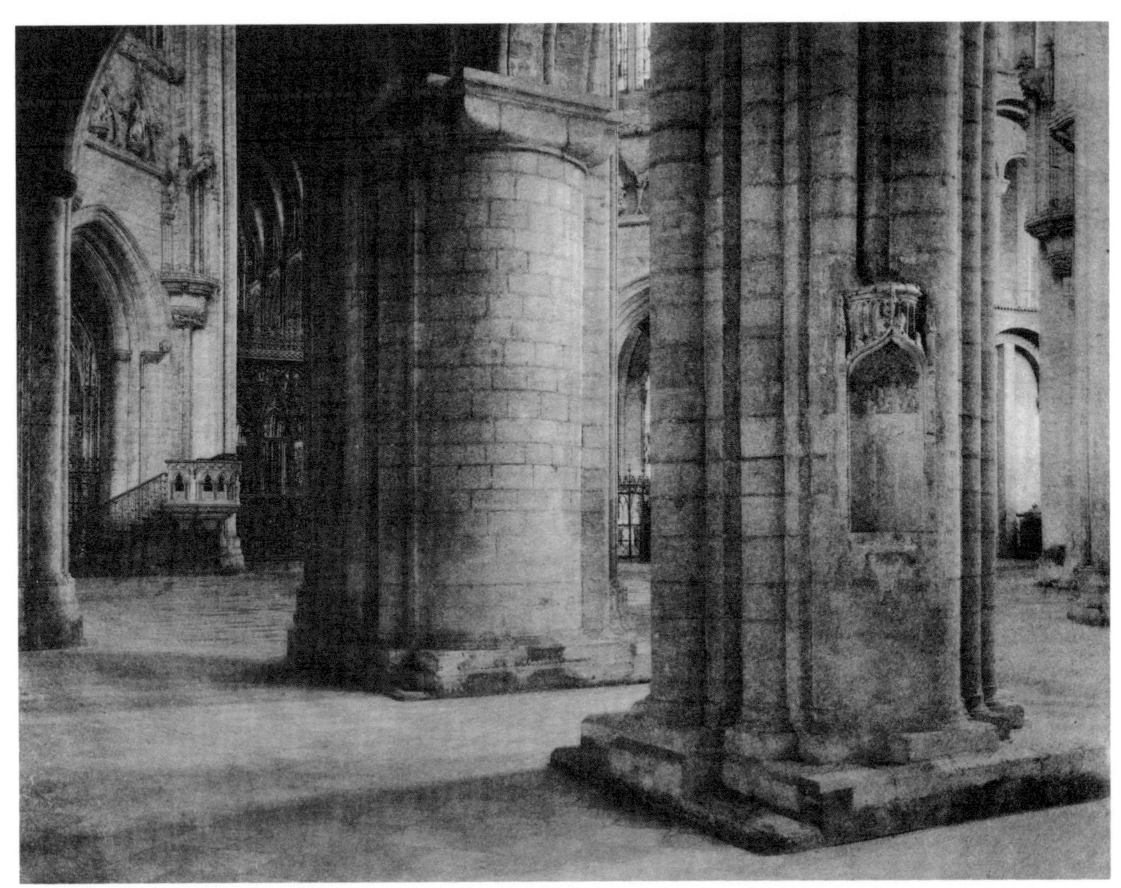

Hugo Henneberg
Austrian, 1863–1918
Villa Falconieri
1900
Camera Work, no. 13 (January 1906)

Hugo Henneberg was a leading Austrian pictorial photographer who became well known in the United States. With Heinrich Kuehn and Hans Watzek, the only other Austrians to be represented in *Camera Work*, he formed a union they called Das Kleeblatt (the Trifolium). The three made trips to other countries together, exhibited as a group, and earned a reputation for their large-scale gum-bichromate prints, some as big as 3 by 4 feet. In *Villa Falconieri*, Henneberg used an exaggerated vertical format and an expansive foreground to create a dramatic pictorial effect. Like much of his other work, this photograph shows his consciousness of the great solemnity of nature. By 1910 Henneberg had apparently turned his artistic attention from photography to painting and relief printing.

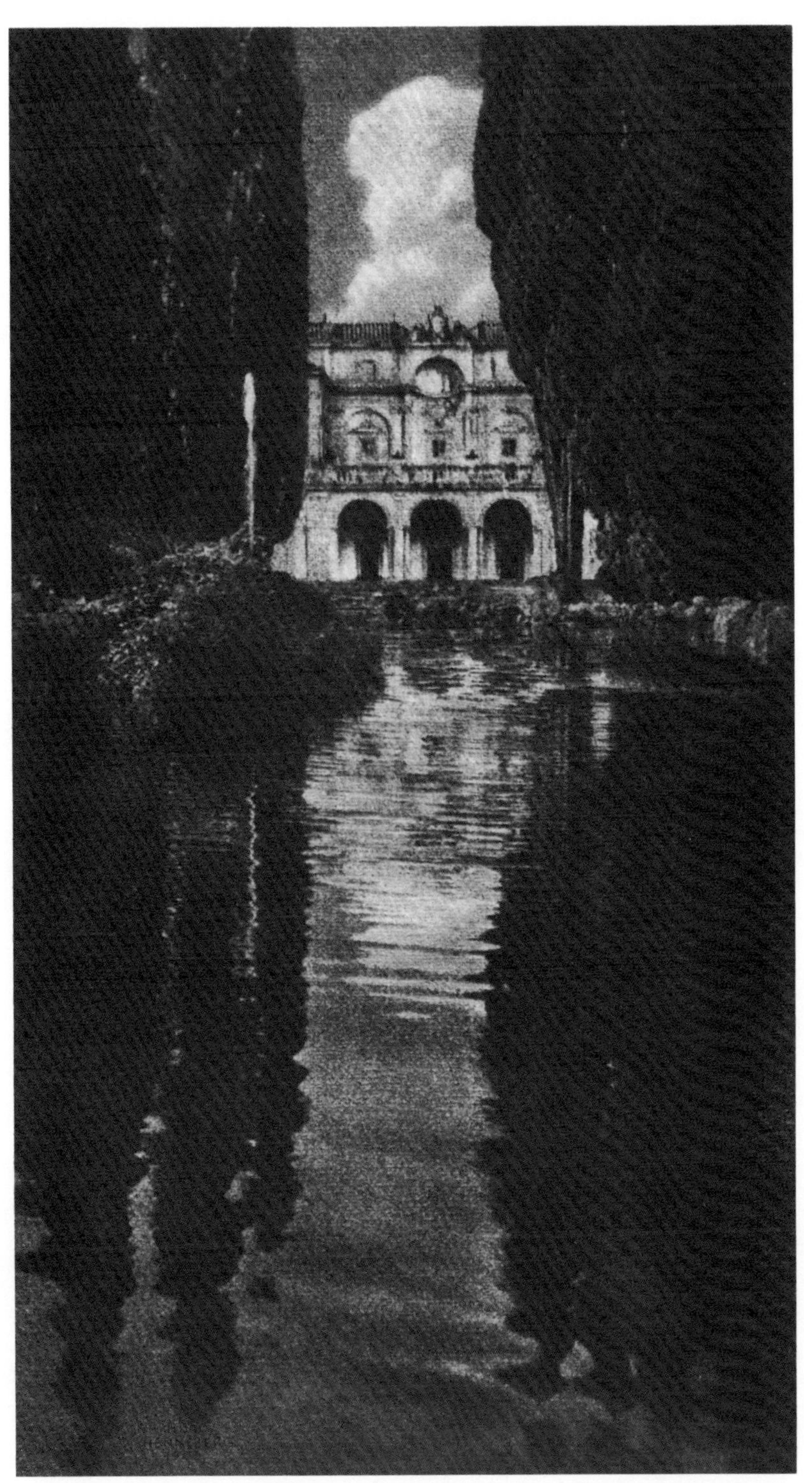

Scottish, 1802–1870 and 1821–1848
Lady Ruthven
c. 1845
Camera Work, no. 11 (April 1905)

The short-lived collaboration of Hill and Adamson is a well-known high
point in the history of portrait photography. From 1843 through 1847,
the team ran a studio in Edinburgh where they produced noble portraits of
striking individuality, which Hill meant to use as studies for a monumental
painting of over four hundred clergymen. Soon, however, they began
photographing the intellectual leaders of their city as well, among them
Lady Ruthven (Mary Campbell, 1789–1885), a friend of Sir Walter Scott's.
Writing in the issue of *Camera Work* in which this unconventional portrait
of Lady Ruthven appeared, J. Craig Annan, who had resurrected Hill and
Adamson's work in the 1890s, detected some humor in the image. "The
pose suggests that it was not chosen for its quaint grace alone, and as a
companion portrait to the full length of her liege lord, who stands in the
orthodox manner, it is distinctly amusing. The Lady herself may have
been, to some extent, responsible for the picture." That Adamson helped
produce the pictures was known at this time—Annan's article briefly
mentioned him—but he was wrongly considered a mere technician, and
Hill received sole credit for the more than twenty images that appeared in
Camera Work.

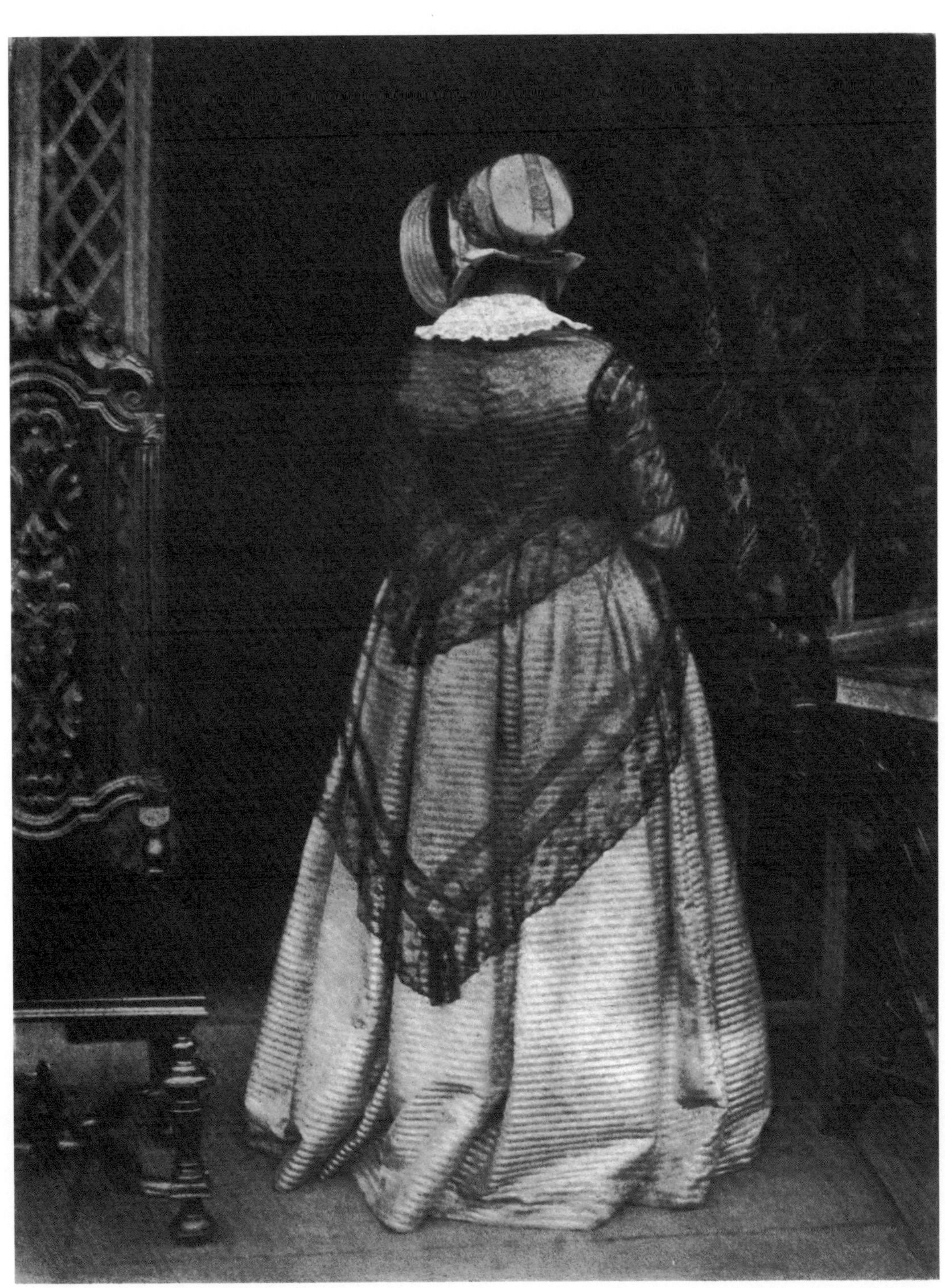

American, 1852–1934
Happy Days
1902
Camera Work, no. 10 (April 1905)

Gertrude Käsebier easily ranks as the foremost woman photographer at
the turn of the century. As a pictorialist, she was a founding member of
Stieglitz's elitist Photo-Secession, and as a commercial photographer, she
maintained a portrait studio in New York for thirty years. The premier
issue of *Camera Work* featured her work, with an appreciation by Charles
H. Caffin in which he observed, "This lady has won a most enviable
reputation both for the quality of the work and for the tact with which
she has united artistic endeavor to business considerations." Much of
Käsebier's work depicts family-related subjects such as the gathering
of children in *Happy Days*—a markedly modern photograph in its flat,
patterned composition and closely cropped image. Käsebier was the first
major Secessionist to become estranged from Stieglitz, and in 1916 she
helped found the rival Pictorial Photographers of America.

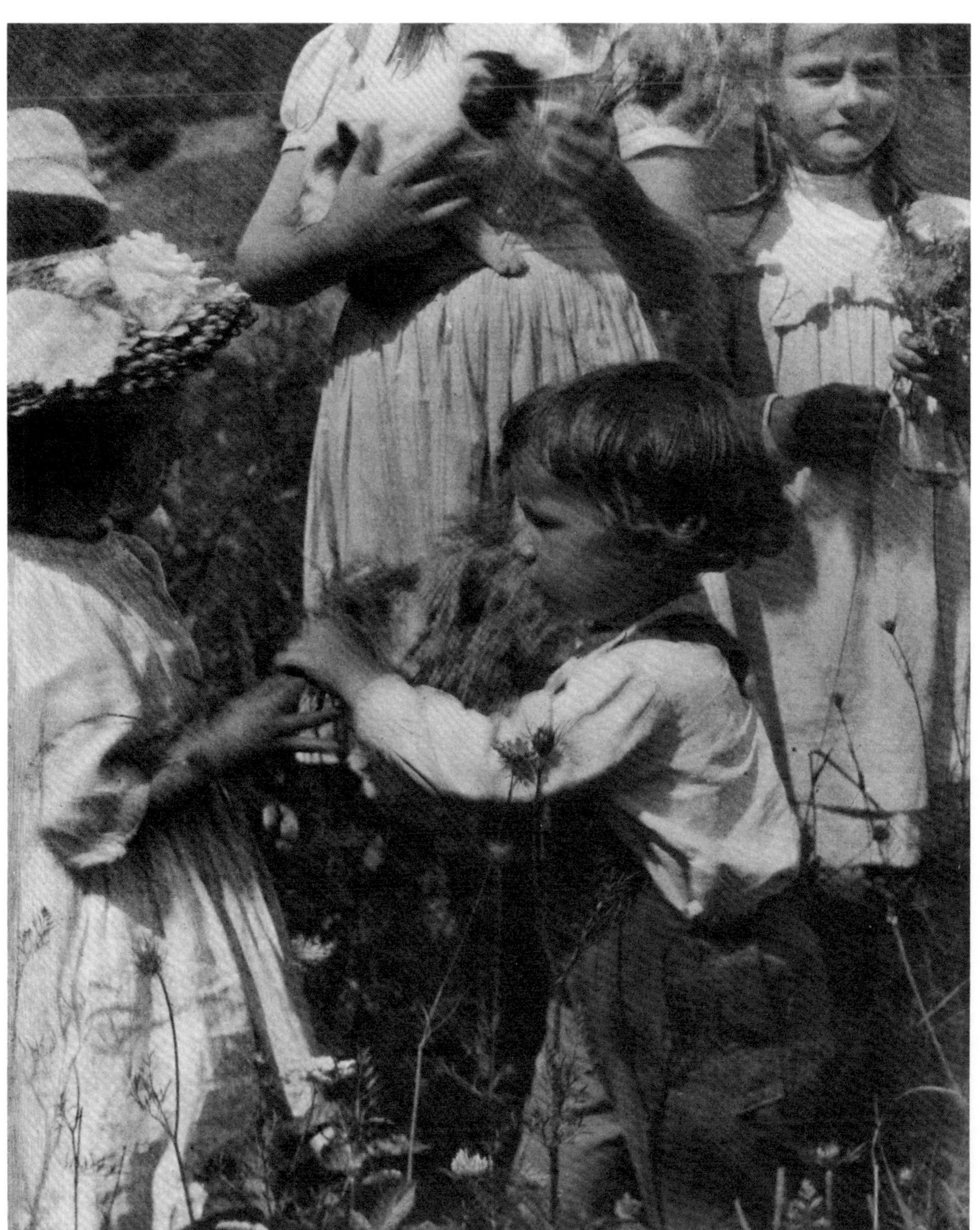

JOSEPH T. KEILEY
American, 1869–1914
Portrait—Miss De C.
1902
Camera Work, no. 17 (January 1907)

Joseph T. Keiley, a lawyer, became Stieglitz's closest friend and ally. Although active as a photographer, Keiley perhaps contributed most significantly to the pictorial movement as a writer. He worked for a few years with Stieglitz on *Camera Notes*, where he gained a reputation for his lengthy articles and exhibition reviews (up to thirty pages), and at *Camera Work* he was the associate editor most involved in the magazine until about 1910. When he died, at the age of 45, he was eulogized at length in the magazine, and his name remained on the masthead until publication ceased. In *Camera Work* number 44, fellow editor J. B. Kerfoot characterized Keiley as "a dreamer of fine dreams who woke to do friendly deeds; a champion of lost causes who could, never-the-less, fight gloriously for obtainable ideals; a glowing intelligence, radiant but diffused when turned on selfish aims, yet capable of keenest focus for others; an enigma and a joy." Among the handful of images by Keiley that appeared in *Camera Work* was this straightforward and elegant portrait of Mercedes de Cordoba (1879–1963), the beautiful wife of the artist Arthur B. Carles.

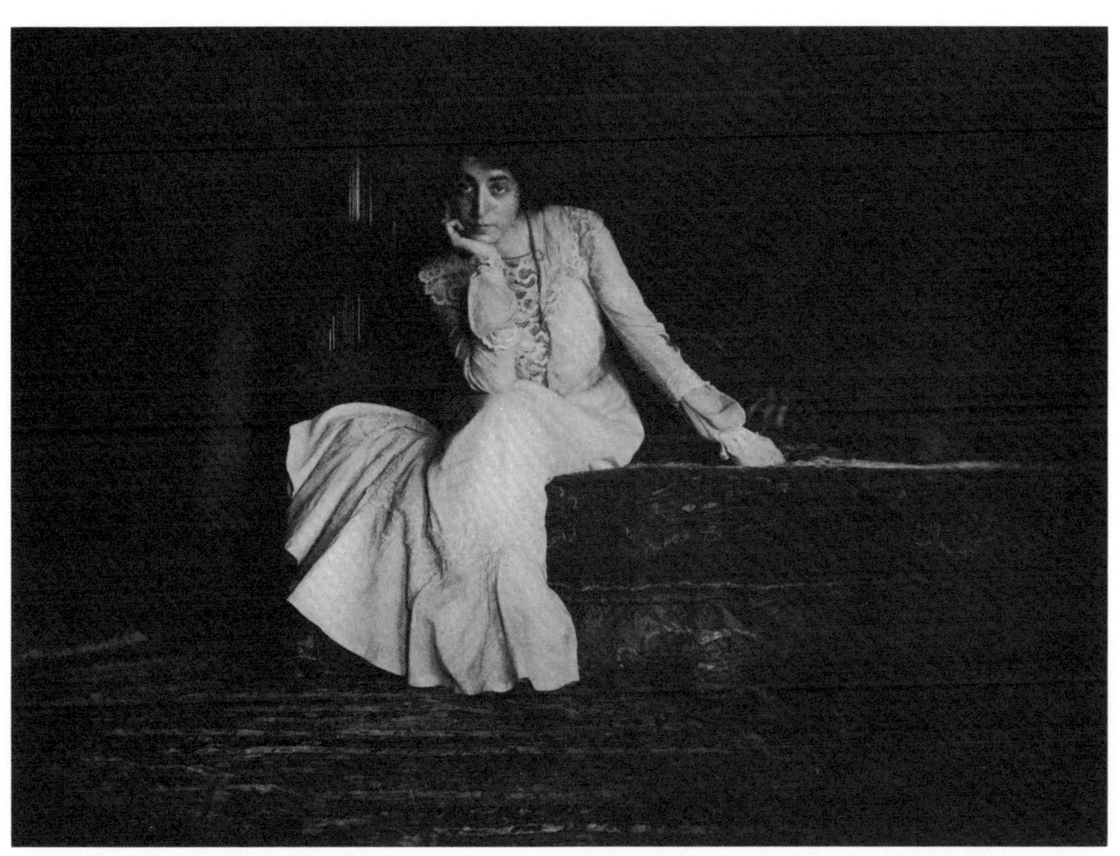

Austrian (b. Germany), 1866–1944
Washerwoman on the Dunes
c. 1905
Camera Work, no. 13 (January 1906)

Heinrich Kuehn (Kühn) led the pictorial movement in Austria and with Hugo Henneberg and Hans Watzek formed the Trifolium in about 1896. The multiple gum-bichromate process that Kuehn adopted was perfectly suited to his landscape imagery of expansive vistas and to the very large prints he liked to make. *Washerwoman on the Dunes*, for instance, an image of great visual spaciousness, exists in gum as a 22-by-28-inch print. By 1910 Kuehn was making his own photogravures, although he never printed any of the illustrations that appeared in the pages of *Camera Work*. The next year Stieglitz devoted an entire issue to Kuehn's work, presenting fifteen images printed by various means: photogravure (hand-printed grain gravures), mezzotint gravure (machine-printed screen gravures), and duplex-halftone (duotones).

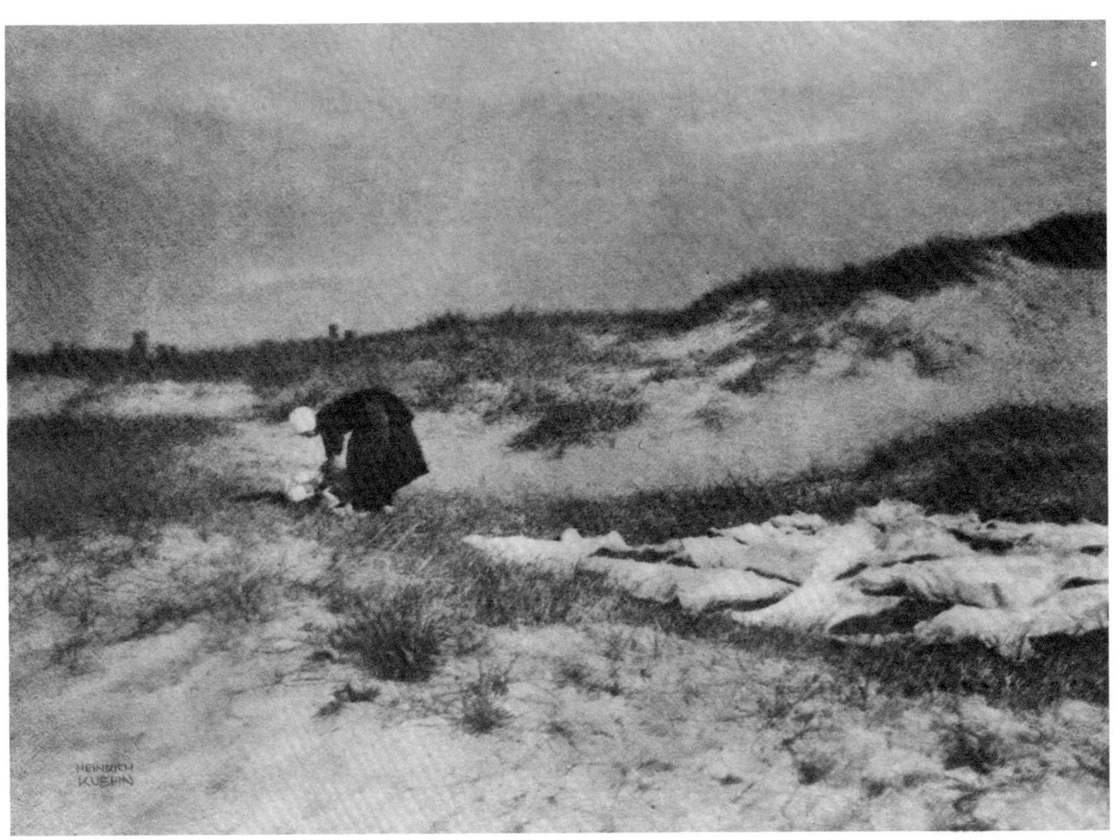
HEINRICH
KUEHN

George H. Seeley
American, 1880–1955
The Firefly
Camera Work, no. 20 (October 1907)

George H. Seeley, almost as young as Alvin Langdon Coburn, was a relative latecomer to the Photo-Secession, joining the group in 1907. The next year he had a one-person exhibition at the Photo-Secession galleries. Charles H. Caffin, sensing the rural influence of Seeley's Stockbridge, Massachusetts, home, wrote in the July 1908 issue of *Camera Work*: "[The] vast silences of nature may be a trifle eerie at times, not seldom awesome, but for the most part spiritually companionable, inviting converse with the abstract and universal. Such impulse, artistically interpreted, makes for symbolism. Form and the color of things, the weavings of light and shade, and vistas of distance, become seen as symbols of spiritual expression. It is in some such vein as this, if I mistake not, that Mr. Seeley views the world and seeks subjects for his pictures." The enigmatic quality of Seeley's work is evident in the otherworldly figure and auras of light in *The Firefly*.

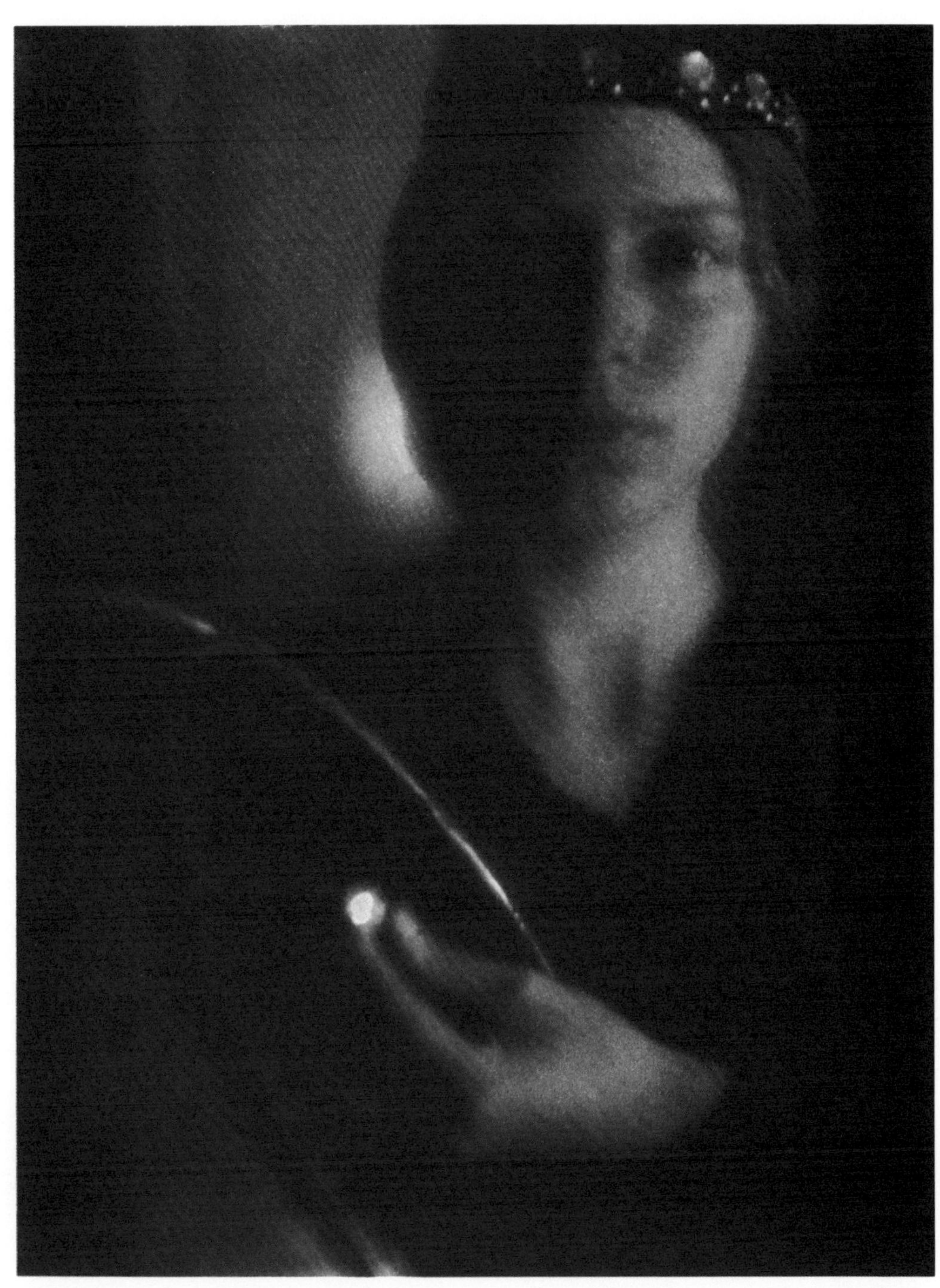

EDWARD STEICHEN
American (b. Luxembourg), 1879–1973
Rodin—Le Penseur
1902
Camera Work, Steichen supplement (April 1906)

Edward Steichen, known as Eduard J. Steichen until World War I, was by far the best-represented photographer in *Camera Work*, with three regular issues and one supplement devoted to his work. Despite their great difference in age, he and Stieglitz became close associates, and Steichen played a key role in the establishment and continuance of both the Photo-Secession galleries (later known as "291") and the quarterly *Camera Work*. In addition to being a photographer, he was a recognized painter (until he gave up painting in 1919) and a close friend of such important European artists as Auguste Rodin, of whom he made many striking portraits. *Rodin—Le Penseur* unites technical virtuosity with psychological insight. Steichen combined two negatives to make a single gum print, producing an image that probes the great sculptor's inner being. After exerting international influence as a turn-of-the-century pictorialist, Steichen went on to a career of unmatched length and variety in the field of photography, which he recounted in his autobiography, *A Life in Photography*.

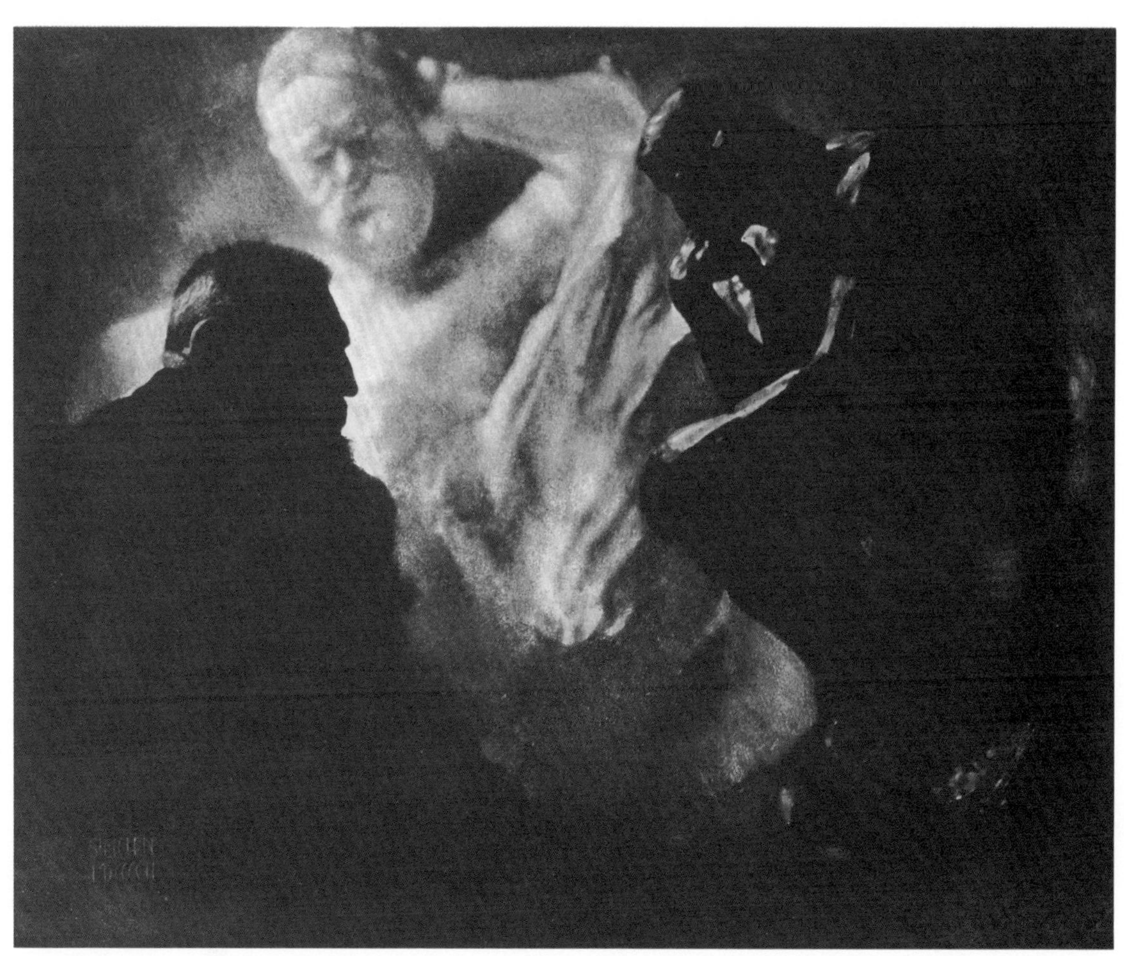

Alfred Stieglitz
American, 1864–1946
Spring Showers, New York
1900
Camera Work, no. 36 (October 1911)

Alfred Stieglitz remains today the uncontested doyen of the photographic world. Through the publications he edited, the galleries he ran, and the sheer force of his own images, he fought to establish photography as a means of creative expression. To advance this cause he also promoted the photogravure process as a method of original printmaking. Among the hundreds of gravures presented in *Camera Work* were Stieglitz's own images, often perfect articulations of his "straight" and radical aesthetic stance. The October 1911 issue contained sixteen remarkable photogravures by Stieglitz, including such classics as *The Steerage*, *The Hand of Man*, and *The Terminal*. The selection closed with the delicate *Spring Showers, New York*. By finding such beauty within the confines of Manhattan, Stieglitz reminded his readers that, to have a chance of succeeding, every creative quest must emanate from the soul.

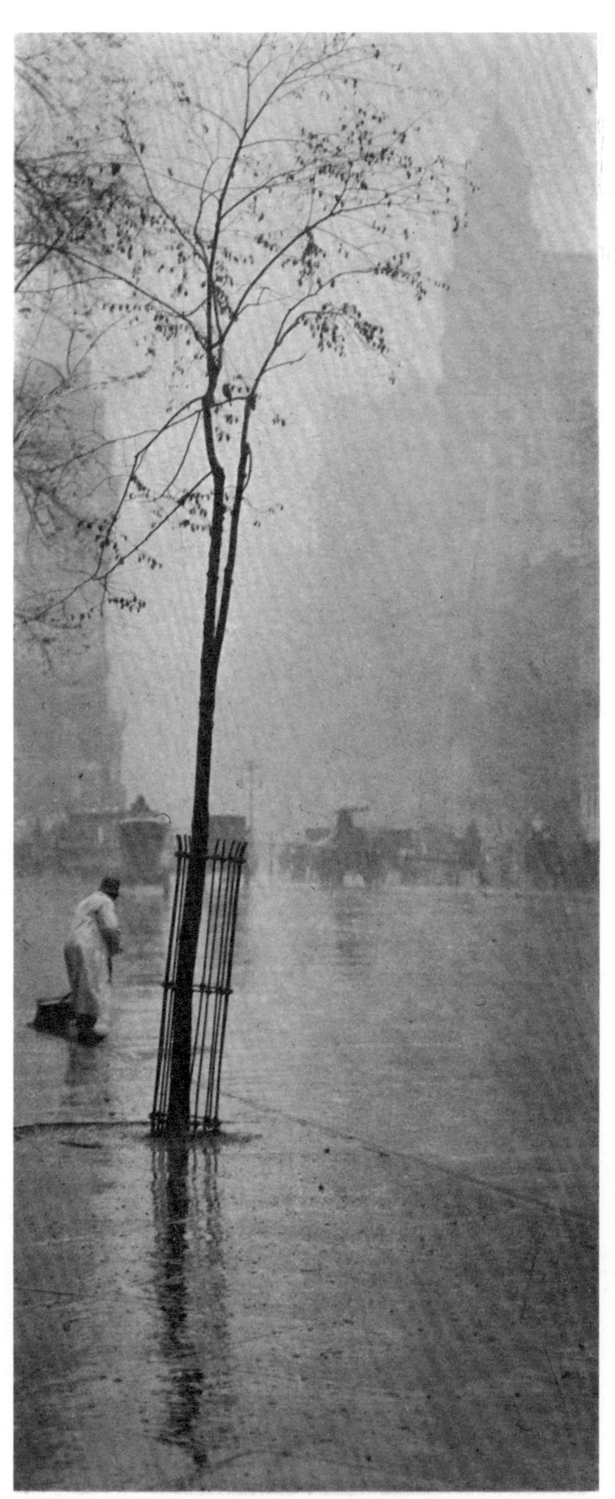

PAUL STRAND
American, 1890–1976
Photograph—New York
1916
Camera Work, no. 49/50 (June 1917)

Paul Strand was the transitional figure in the shift from pictorialism to the "straight" approach in creative American photography. In 1915 he abandoned soft-focus effects, at Stieglitz's urging, and began making images with a directness and purity considered inherent in the photographic medium. Among the earliest were street portraits, including this one, which evidenced the strong social and humanistic consciousness that characterized Strand's work throughout his long career. He wrote in the last issue of *Camera Work* (where this image appeared), "Photography is only a new road from a different direction but moving toward the common goal, which is Life." In addition to contributing gravures to *Camera Work*, Strand issued his 1942 *Mexican Portfolio* as a limited-edition set of hand-printed photogravures.

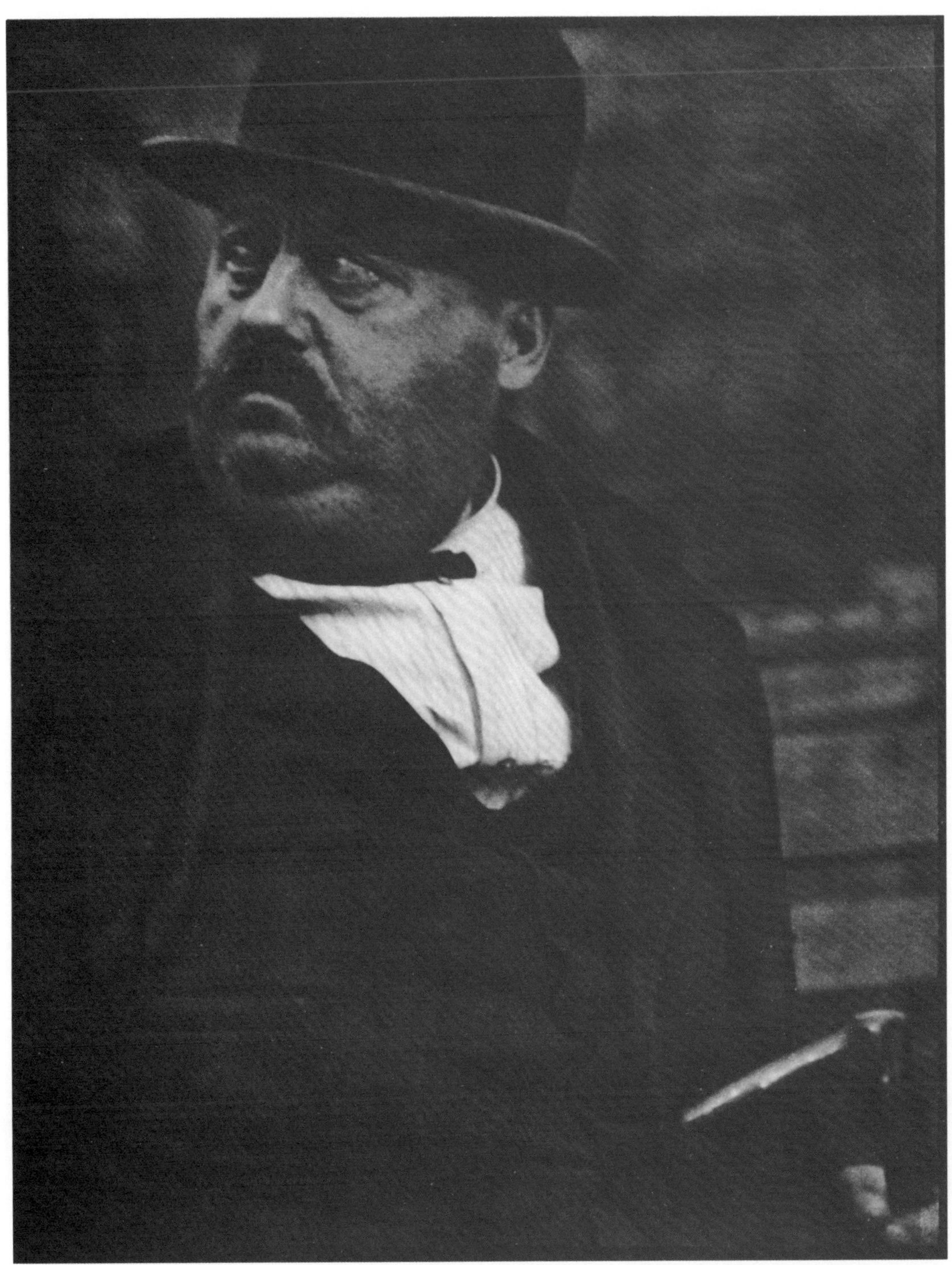

Clarence H. White was a gentle midwesterner with a pictorial sensitivity
unusual even among the Photo-Secessionists. Although he moved from
Newark, Ohio, to New York City in 1906, his imagery remained quiet and
centered on his family. In the issue of *Camera Work* in which the soft-focus
and formalistic *Drops of Rain* appeared, Charles H. Caffin observed: "It is
[the] rare combination of a natural instinct for beauty, refined and trained
by an impulse from within, and of an imagination, pure and serious, that
gives to all White's work not only a pronounced individuality, but also
a peculiarly rarified charm. They are the emanations of a beautiful spirit."
Along with Gertrude Käsebier, White helped organize the Pictorial
Photographers of America after the Photo-Secession began to break up.
In 1914 he established the Clarence H. White School of Photography,
giving classes in Maine and New York, and soon became widely acclaimed
as a teacher.

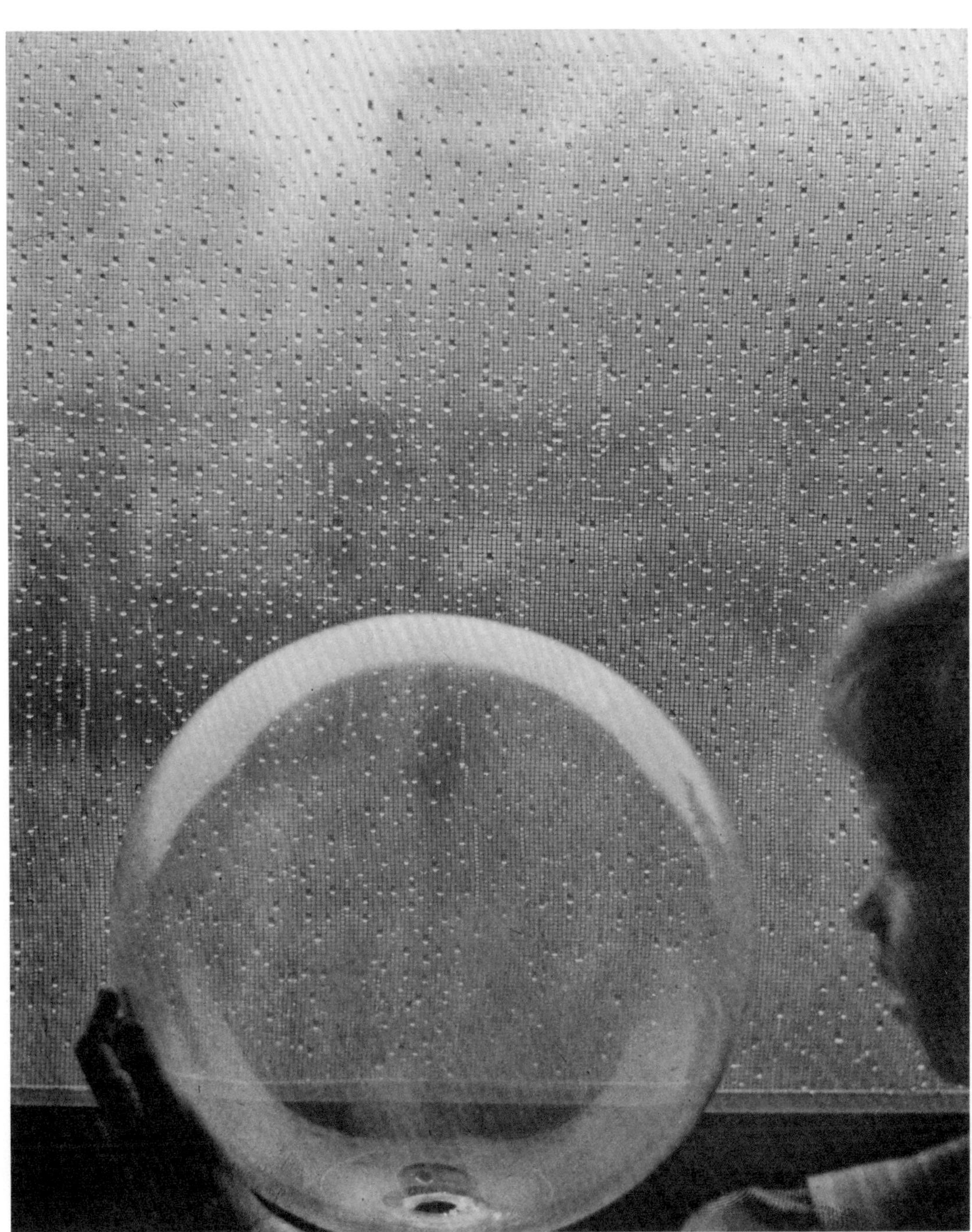

Photographers Represented in *Camera Work*

This list includes all the photographers whose work appeared in *Camera Work*. The number of photographic images by each, printed in the magazine by photogravure, halftone, and other processes, follows the name.

Abbott, C. Yarnall (3)
Adamson, Prescott (1)
Annan, J. Craig (25)
Becher, Arthur E. (1)
Boughton, Alice (6)
Brigman, Anne W. (11)
Bruguière, Francis (1)
Cadby, William A. (2)
Cameron, Julia Margaret (5)
Coburn, Alvin Langdon (26)
Davison, George (8)
Demachy, Robert (16)
De Meyer, Adolf (21)
Devens, Mary (1)
Dugmore, A. Radclyffe (2)
Dyer, William B. (2)
Eugene, Frank (28)
Evans, Frederick H. (7)
French, Herbert G. (5)
Haviland, Paul B. (9)
Henneberg, Hugo (3)
Herzog, F. Benedict (5)
Hill, David Octavius, and
    Robert Adamson (21)
Hinton, A. Horsley (2)
Hofmeister, Theodor and Oscar (6)
Käsebier, Gertrude (12)
Keiley, Joseph T. (7)

Kernochan, Marshall R. (1)
Kuehn, Heinrich (19)
Lamb, H. Mortimer (1)
Le Bègue, Renée (2)
Lewis, Arthur Allen (1)
Muir, Ward (2)
Post, William B. (1)
Pratt, Frederick H. (1)
Puyo, Constant (3)
Renwick, William W. (1)
Rey, Guido (2)
Rubincam, Harry C. (1)
Sears, Sarah C. (2)
Seeley, George H. (18)
Shaw, George Bernard (1)
Spencer, Ema (1)
Steichen, Edward (68)
Stieglitz, Alfred (47)
Strand, Paul (17)
Strauss, John Francis (1)
Struss, Karl F. (8)
Watson-Schütze, Eva (4)
Watzek, Hans (5)
White, Clarence H. (27)
White, Clarence H., and
    Alfred Stieglitz (4)
Wilmerding, William E. (1)

THE PHOTOGRAVURE PROCESS

PHOTOGRAVURE IS A PHOTOMECHANICAL PROCESS by which photographic images are printed in ink. As intaglio prints, photogravures bear some resemblance to etchings and engravings, but they are differentiated from these handmade prints by the use of camera-generated images and light-sensitive materials for platemaking. The origins of the process go back to the very beginnings of photography. The inventors Joseph-Nicéphore Niepce and William Henry Fox Talbot, in their efforts to secure fixed images from nature, each independently made what amounted to photoetchings.

As early as 1814, Niepce had begun experimenting with light-sensitive varnishes for use in the new art of lithography. But his landmark success came twelve years later, when he reproduced the engraved portrait of Cardinal d'Amboise from a pewter heliographic plate. To do this, he first coated a pewter plate with bitumen of Judea, a light-sensitive asphalt. Then he put the sensitized plate in contact with the original engraving (which had been oiled to make it translucent) and placed it in sunlight. After an exposure of several hours the bitumen under the clear areas of the image hardened and became resistant to the acid bath, which was the next step. The acid etched only the unhardened areas—those corresponding to the dark areas of the image. Niepce then washed the plate and had it printed by the traditional intaglio method.

Talbot's contribution consisted of two new developments in the process, which he patented in 1852. The first was his discovery that gelatin treated with potassium bichromate hardened when exposed to light. In subsequent refinements of the photogravure process, this material was used as the acid resist in place of Niepce's bitumen of Judea. Talbot's second contribution was his recognition that some sort of screen was needed to break up the image area. While Niepce's portrait of Cardinal d'Amboise was produced from an engraving and so already had a linear structure, Talbot's images made directly from nature required a network of lines so that large etched areas of the plate would hold ink. At first he introduced a gauze mesh (his "photographic veil") that gave the plate a screen pattern over which he laid objects like fern leaves and exposed them to light. In 1858, he improved this technique by dusting the plate with a copal powder to give the image a finer and more even screen tint. At this time he also began using transparencies of his camera images to make prints that he called photoglyphic engravings.

The photogravure process originated in Talbot's work, but the technique used in *Camera Work* was devised in 1879 by Karl Klič, a Czechoslovakian painter living in Vienna. Keeping his process secret, Klič sold licenses for its use to such well-known firms as T. and R. Annan and Sons (Glasgow), [Adolphe] Braun et Compagnie (Paris), and the F. Bruckmann Verlag

[77]

(Munich). By 1886, however, the process had been published in full detail, and to this day it remains essentially unchanged.

The first procedure in making a photogravure print is the preparation of a printing plate. This plate, made of pure copper, must be thoroughly cleaned, its surface highly polished, and its edges beveled (so the paper will not be cut during printing). Next, it is evenly dusted or sprayed with an acid resist of resin or bitumen, to give it a tooth, and heated to make the resist adhere. Since this procedure is identical to the preparation of aquatint plates, early photogravure was sometimes called photoaquatint.

While the plate is being readied, the image can also be prepared. A positive transparency is made from either the original negative or a copy negative. This transparency, which must be made the size desired for the final print, is then contact printed to a sheet of gravure or carbon tissue, a paper coated with gelatin, bichromate, and pigment.

All that remains, before going to press, is the transfer of the image to the prepared copper plate. The image-carrying tissue and the plate are sandwiched together under pressure and soaked in water, and the paper backing of the tissue is removed. Portions of the gelatin that received little or no light during exposure to the transparency remain soluble and are washed away, leaving a gelatin image that will act as a resist when the plate is etched. Placed in a succession of acid baths, the plate is bitten in proportion to the thickness of the gelatin coating, so that a multitude of minute depressions of varying depths are produced. During printing, the deeper cells will hold more ink and thus transfer more ink to the paper, creating the darker areas of the image.

Finally, after the plate has been thoroughly washed (and steel-faced, for editions of over fifty), the gravures can be printed—one by one on an etching press, like all other forms of intaglio hand printing. First, a stiff ink is applied to the entire plate and worked into the recessed areas that form the image. Next, the surface of the plate is wiped clean, so that ink remains only in the hollowed-out portions. The plate is then laid face up on a small flatbed press, and a piece of dampened high-quality paper (Japan tissue, in the case of *Camera Work*) is placed on top of it along with protective pads. When run through the press, the paper is forced into the small depressions that hold the ink and the image is transferred. To make the next impression, the plate must be cleaned and the entire process repeated.

Because photogravure is very time-consuming, its use today is limited, but its industrial sister, rotogravure, is fairly widely practiced. Also developed by Karl Klič in the late nineteenth century, this process utilizes a regular screen (different from the halftone screen) and cylindrical plates. Sometimes referred to as screen gravure, rotogravure printing is economical only for very large press runs, and its high-quality reproductions can be seen in Sunday newspaper picture magazines and *National Geographic*.

SELECTED BIBLIOGRAPHY

Brandau, Robert, editor. *De Meyer.* Alfred A. Knopf, New York, 1976.

Bry, Doris. *Alfred Stieglitz: Photographer.* Museum of Fine Arts, Boston, 1965.

Caffin, Charles H. *Photography as a Fine Art.* Doubleday, Page and Company, New York, 1901. Reprint. Morgan and Morgan, Hastings-on-Hudson, N.Y., 1971.

Camera Notes. Edited by Alfred Stieglitz. The Camera Club, New York, 1897–1903.

Camera Work. Edited and published by Alfred Stieglitz. New York, 1903–1917.

Coburn, Alvin Langdon. *Alvin Langdon Coburn, Photographer: An Autobiography.* Edited by Helmut and Alison Gernsheim. Frederick A. Praeger, New York, 1966. Reprint. Dover Publications, New York, 1978.

Corn, Wanda M. *The Color of Mood: American Tonalism, 1880–1910.* M. H. de Young Memorial Museum and California Palace of the Legion of Honor, San Francisco, 1972.

Crawford, William. *The Keepers of Light: A History and Working Guide to Early Photographic Processes.* Morgan and Morgan, Dobbs Ferry, N.Y., 1979.

Denison, Herbert. *A Treatise on Photogravure in Intaglio by the Talbot-Klic Process.* Iliffe and Son, London, 1895. Reprint. Visual Studies Workshop, Rochester, N.Y., 1974.

Doty, Robert. *Photo-Secession: Photography as a Fine Art.* George Eastman House, Rochester, N.Y., 1960. Reprint. Dover Publications, New York, 1978.

Frank, Waldo, Lewis Mumford, Dorothy Norman, Paul Rosenfeld, and Harold Ruggs, editors. *America and Alfred Stieglitz: A Collective Portrait.* Doubleday, Doran and Company, Garden City, N.Y., 1934. Reprint. Aperture, Millerton, N.Y., 1979.

Glasgow Portraits by J. Craig Annan (1864–1946), Photographer. Scottish Arts Council, Edinburgh, 1967.

Green, Jonathan, editor. *"Camera Work": A Critical Anthology.* Aperture, Millerton, N.Y., 1973.

Greenough, Sarah, and Juan Hamilton. *Alfred Stieglitz: Photographs and Writings.* National Gallery of Art, Washington, D.C., 1983.

Harker, Margaret F. *The Linked Ring: The Secession Movement in Photography in Britain, 1892–1910.* Royal Photographic Society and William Heinemann, London, 1979.

Hartmann, Sadakichi. *The Valiant Knights of Daguerre: Selected Critical Essays on Photography and Profiles of Photographic Pioneers.* Edited by Harry W. Lawton and George Knox. University of California Press, Berkeley, 1978.

Heyman, Terese Thau. *Anne Brigman: Pictorial Photographer/Pagan/Member of the Photo-Secession.* Oakland Museum, Oakland, Calif., 1974.

Homer, William Innes. *A Pictorial Heritage: The Photographs of Gertrude Käsebier.* Delaware Art Museum, Wilmington, 1979.

———. *Alfred Stieglitz and the Photo-Secession.* New York Graphic Society. Little, Brown and Company, Boston, 1983.

Hull, Robert Piatt. *"Camera Work": An American Quarterly.* Ph.D. dissertation, Northwestern University, 1970. (University Microfilms International, Ann Arbor, Mich.)

Jay, Bill. *Robert Demachy, 1859–1936: Photographs and Essays.* Academy Editions, London, and St. Martin's Press, New York, 1974.

Jussim, Estelle. *Visual Communication and the Graphic Arts: Photographic Technologies in the Nineteenth Century.* R. R. Bowker Company, New York, 1974.

———. "Technology or Aesthetics: Alfred Stieglitz and Photogravure." *History of Photography*, January 1979 (vol. 3, no. 1), pp. 81–92.

Longwell, Dennis. *Steichen: The Master Prints, 1895–1914: The Symbolist Period.* Museum of Modern Art, New York, 1978.

Lowe, Sue Davidson. *Stieglitz: A Memoir/Biography.* Farrar, Straus and Giroux, New York, 1983.

Margolis, Marianne Fulton, editor. *"Camera Work": A Pictorial Guide.* Dover Publications, New York, 1978.

Naef, Weston J. *The Collection of Alfred Stieglitz: Fifty Pioneers of Modern Photography.* Metropolitan Museum of Art and Viking Press, New York, 1978.

Newhall, Beaumont. *Frederick H. Evans: Photographer of the Majesty, Light and Space of the Medieval Cathedrals of England and France.* Aperture, Millerton, N.Y., 1973.

———. *The History of Photography: From 1839 to the Present.* [Fifth edition]. Museum of Modern Art, New York, 1982.

Newhall, Nancy. *P. H. Emerson: The Fight for Photography as a Fine Art.* Aperture, Millerton, N.Y., 1975.

Norman, Dorothy. *Alfred Stieglitz: An American Seer.* Random House, New York, 1973.

Photo-Secession. Catalogue 6. Lunn Gallery / Graphics International, Washington, D.C., 1978.

Seligman, Herbert J. *Alfred Stieglitz Talking.* Yale University Library, New Haven, Conn., 1966.

Steichen, Edward. *A Life in Photography.* Doubleday and Company, Garden City, N.Y., 1963.

Stieglitz, Alfred. "Four Happenings." *Twice a Year*, Fall/Winter 1942 (no. 8/9), pp. 105–136.

Stieglitz Letters. Alfred Stieglitz Archive. Collection of American Literature. Beinecke Rare Book and Manuscript Library, Yale University, New Haven, Conn.

Symbolism of Light: The Photographs of Clarence H. White. Delaware Art Museum, Wilmington, 1977.

EXHIBITION CHECKLIST

Dimensions given are for image area; height precedes width. Illustrated photographs are noted with an asterisk.

1. Cover of *Camera Work**
   No. 3 (July 1903)
   Letterpress
   12×9 in. (30.5×22.5 cm)
   The Minneapolis Institute of Arts,
     gift of Julia Marshall

J. CRAIG ANNAN
Scottish, 1864–1946

2. *The Etching Printer*
   1902
   Gelatin silver print
   10¾×13¹⁵⁄₁₆ in. (27.4×35.8 cm)
   The Metropolitan Museum of Art,
     Alfred Stieglitz Collection

3. *The Etching Printer—William
     Strang, Esq., A.R.A.**
   Camera Work, no. 19 (July 1907)
   Photogravure
   5¹⁵⁄₁₆×7¾ in. (15.1×19.7 cm)
   The Minneapolis Institute of Arts,
     gift of Julia Marshall

ANNE W. BRIGMAN
American, 1869–1950

4. *The Source*
   c. 1906
   Gelatin silver print
   9⁷⁄₁₆×5½ in. (23.9×14.0 cm)
   The Metropolitan Museum of Art,
     Alfred Stieglitz Collection

5. *The Source**
   Camera Work, no. 25
     (January 1909)
   Photogravure
   9¼×5⁷⁄₁₆ in. (23.5×13.9 cm)
   The Minneapolis Institute of Arts,
     gift of Julia Marshall

JULIA MARGARET CAMERON
English (b. India), 1815–1879

6. *Thomas Carlyle*
   1867
   Albumen print
   12½×9½ in. (31.8×24.1 cm)
   Vassar College Art Gallery,
     gift of Lydia Evans Tunnard

7. *Carlyle**
   Camera Work, no. 41
     (January 1913)
   Photogravure
   8½×6¼ in. (21.7×15.9 cm)
   The Minneapolis Institute of Arts,
     gift of Julia Marshall

ALVIN LANGDON COBURN
English (b. United States),
   1882–1966

8. *The Bridge—London*
   c. 1903
   Gum-bichromate over platinum
     print
   10¹⁵⁄₁₆×8⅝ in. (27.9×22.0 cm)
   Collection of the International
     Museum of Photography at
     George Eastman House

9. *The Bridge—London**
Camera Work, no. 15 (July 1906)
Photogravure
8 × 6⅜ in. (20.3 × 16.2 cm)
The Minneapolis Institute of Arts,
gift of Julia Marshall

ROBERT DEMACHY
French, 1859-1936

10. *La Vallée de la Touques, No. 2*
1902
Gum-bichromate print
6¹³⁄₁₆ × 8¹³⁄₁₆ in. (17.3 × 22.4 cm)
The Metropolitan Museum of Art,
Alfred Stieglitz Collection

11. *Toucques Valley**
Camera Work, no. 16
(October 1906)
Photogravure
6³⁄₁₆ × 8⅛₆ in. (15.7 × 20.5 cm)
The Minneapolis Institute of Arts,
gift of Julia Marshall

ADOLF DE MEYER
American (b. France), 1868-1946

12. *Hydrangea*
c. 1908
Platinum print
13⅛ × 10¹³⁄₁₆ in. (33.4 × 27.5 cm)
The Royal Photographic Society,
gift of Alvin Langdon Coburn

13. *Still Life**
Camera Work, no. 24
(October 1908)
Photogravure
7⁹⁄₁₆ × 6⅛ in. (19.3 × 15.6 cm)
The Minneapolis Institute of Arts,
gift of Julia Marshall

WILLIAM B. DYER
American, 1860-1931

14. *L'Allegro*
1902
Gum-bichromate print
12⅝ × 6¹¹⁄₁₆ in. (32.0 × 16.9 cm)
The Metropolitan Museum of Art,
Alfred Stieglitz Collection

15. *L'Allegro**
Camera Work, no. 18 (April 1907)
Photogravure
8½ × 4½ in. (21.7 × 11.4 cm)
The Minneapolis Institute of Arts,
gift of Julia Marshall

FRANK EUGENE
German (b. United States),
1865-1936

16. *Dido*
1898
Gelatin silver print
10 × 14¼ in. (25.3 × 36.1 cm)
The Metropolitan Museum of Art,
Alfred Stieglitz Collection

17. *La Cigale*
Camera Work, no. 5 (January 1904)
Photogravure
4¹³⁄₁₆ × 6¾ in. (12.2 × 17.1 cm)
The Minneapolis Institute of Arts,
gift of Julia Marshall

18. *Lady of Charlotte*
c. 1899
Platinum print
4¼ × 3⅞ in. (10.8 × 7.8 cm)
The Metropolitan Museum of Art,
Alfred Stieglitz Collection

19. *Lady of Charlotte**
Camera Work, no. 25
(January 1909)
Photogravure
4½ × 3⁵⁄₁₆ in. (11.5 × 8.4 cm)
The Minneapolis Institute of Arts,
gift of Julia Marshall

20. *Portrait of Alfred Stieglitz*
1907
Platinum print
6⅝×4¹³/₁₆ in. (16.9×12.2 cm)
The Art Institute of Chicago,
   Alfred Stieglitz Collection

21. *Mr. Alfred Stieglitz* *
Camera Work, no. 25
   (January 1909)
Photogravure
6½×4⁷/₁₆ in. (16.5×11.4 cm)
The Minneapolis Institute of Arts,
   gift of Julia Marshall

FREDERICK H. EVANS
English, 1853–1943

22. *Ely Cathedral, "The Strength of
   the Normans"*
1903
Platinum print
7¼×9¼ in. (18.4×23.5 cm)
Collection of the International
   Museum of Photography at
   George Eastman House

23. *Ely Cathedral: Across Nave
   and Octagon* *
Camera Work, no. 4
   (October 1903)
Photogravure
5¾×7⁵/₁₆ in. (14.7×18.6 cm)
The Minneapolis Institute of Arts,
   gift of Julia Marshall

HUGO HENNEBERG
Austrian, 1863–1918

24. *Villa Falconieri, Frascati*
1900
Gum-bichromate print
27⁷/₁₆×15 in. (69.7×37.9 cm)
The Metropolitan Museum of Art,
   Alfred Stieglitz Collection

25. *Villa Falconieri* *
Camera Work, no. 13
   (January 1906)
Photogravure
9⅜×5 in. (23.9×12.8 cm)
The Minneapolis Institute of Arts,
   gift of Julia Marshall

DAVID OCTAVIUS HILL and
ROBERT ADAMSON
Scottish, 1802–1870 and 1821–1848

26. *Lady Ruthven*
c. 1845
Salt print from paper negative
8¹/₁₆×6⁵/₁₆ in. (20.4×16.0 cm)
Collection of the International
   Museum of Photography at
   George Eastman House

27. *Lady Ruthven* *
Camera Work, no. 11 (April 1905)
Photogravure
7⅞×5⅞ in. (20.0×14.9 cm)
The Minneapolis Institute of Arts,
   William Hood Dunwoody Fund

28. *J. Henning and Handyside
   Ritchie*
c. 1844
Salt print from paper negative
9¼×6¹³/₁₆ in. (23.5×17.3 cm)
The Museum of Modern Art,
   New York, gift of Warner
   Communications, Inc.

29. *Handyside Ritchie and
   Wm. Henning*
Camera Work, no. 37
   (January 1912)
Photogravure
8⅜×6¼ in. (21.4×15.9 cm)
The Minneapolis Institute of Arts,
   gift of Julia Marshall

GERTRUDE KÄSEBIER
American, 1852-1934

30. *The Manger*
1899
Platinum print
13³⁄₁₆ × 9¹¹⁄₁₆ in. (33.5 × 24.6 cm)
The Art Institute of Chicago,
  gift of Mina Turner

31. *The Manger*
Camera Work, no. 1 (January 1903)
Photogravure
8⅜ × 5⅞ in. (21.3 × 14.9 cm)
The Minneapolis Institute of Arts,
  gift of Julia Marshall

32. *Blessed Art Thou among Women*
1899
Platinum print
9⅝ × 7⅝ in. (24.5 × 19.5 cm)
Collection of the International
  Museum of Photography at
  George Eastman House

33. *Blessed Art Thou among Women*
Camera Work, no. 1 (January 1903)
Photogravure
9⁵⁄₁₆ × 5⁵⁄₁₆ in. (23.7 × 14.2 cm)
The Minneapolis Institute of Arts,
  gift of Julia Marshall

34. *Happy Days*
1902
Gum-bichromate print
12½ × 9¾ in. (40.8 × 24.7 cm)
The Museum of Modern Art,
  New York, gift of
  Hermine M. Turner

35. *Happy Days* *
Camera Work, no. 10 (April 1905)
Photogravure
7¾ × 6⅛ in. (19.7 × 15.7 cm)
The Minneapolis Institute of Arts,
  gift of Julia Marshall

JOSEPH T. KEILEY
American, 1869-1914

36. *Miss de C.*
1902
Platinum print
3⅜ × 4½ in. (8.6 × 11.4 cm)
The Metropolitan Museum of Art,
  Alfred Stieglitz Collection

37. *Portrait—Miss De C.* *
Camera Work, no. 17
  (January 1907)
Photogravure
4¾ × 6⁵⁄₁₆ in. (12.0 × 16.0 cm)
The Minneapolis Institute of Arts,
  gift of Julia Marshall

HEINRICH KUEHN
Austrian (b. Germany), 1866-1944

38. *Wäscherin in der Düne*
c. 1905
Gum-bichromate print
21¾ × 28¹¹⁄₁₆ in. (55.4 × 72.9 cm)
The Metropolitan Museum of Art,
  Alfred Stieglitz Collection

39. *Washerwoman on the Dunes* *
Camera Work, no. 13
  (January 1906)
Photogravure
6⅝ × 9 in. (16.9 × 22.8 cm)
The Minneapolis Institute of Arts,
  gift of Julia Marshall

GEORGE H. SEELEY
American, 1880-1955

40. *The Glow Worm*
n.d.
Platinum print
9⁷⁄₁₆ × 7¹¹⁄₁₆ in. (24.3 × 19.5 cm)
The Royal Photographic Society,
  gift of Alvin Langdon Coburn

41. *The Firefly**
    Camera Work, no. 20
      (October 1907)
    Photogravure
    7¹⁵⁄₁₆ × 6¼ in. (20.2 × 15.8 cm)
    The Minneapolis Institute of Arts,
      gift of Julia Marshall

American (b. Luxembourg),
1879–1973

42. *Self-portrait*
    1902
    Gum-bichromate print
    10½ × 7⅞ in. (26.7 × 20.0 cm)
    The Art Institute of Chicago,
      Alfred Stieglitz Collection

43. *Self-Portrait*
    Camera Work, no. 2 (April 1903)
    Photogravure
    8⁷⁄₁₆ × 6⅜ in. (21.5 × 16.3 cm)
    The Minneapolis Institute of Arts,
      William Hood Dunwoody Fund

44. *Rodin—Le Penseur*
    1902
    Gum-bichromate print
    10⁵⁄₁₆ × 12¹³⁄₁₆ in. (26.2 × 32.5 cm)
    The Art Institute of Chicago,
      Alfred Stieglitz Collection

45. *Rodin—Le Penseur**
    Camera Work, Steichen
      supplement (April 1906)
    Photogravure
    6¹⁄₁₆ × 7¼ in. (15.4 × 18.7 cm)
    The Minneapolis Institute of Arts,
      gift of Julia Marshall

46. *J. P. Morgan*
    1903
    Gelatin silver print by
      Rolf Petersen
    16⁹⁄₁₆ × 13⅜ in. (42.0 × 34.0 cm)
    The Museum of Modern Art,
      New York, gift of the
      photographer

47. *J. Pierpont Morgan, Esq.*
    Camera Work, Steichen
      supplement (April 1906)
    Photogravure
    8¹⁄₁₆ × 6³⁄₁₆ in. (20.5 × 15.7 cm)
    The Minneapolis Institute of Arts,
      gift of Julia Marshall

48. *The Pond—Moonrise*
    1903
    Platinum print, toned
    15⅝ × 19 in. (39.7 × 48.2 cm)
    The Metropolitan Museum of Art,
      Alfred Stieglitz Collection

49. *Moonlight: The Pond*
    Camera Work, no. 14
      (April 1906)
    Photogravure
    6⅜ × 8 in. (16.2 × 20.3 cm)
    The Minneapolis Institute of Arts,
      gift of Julia Marshall

American, 1864–1946

50. *The Terminal*
    1892
    Chloride print
    4¼ × 3⁹⁄₁₆ in. (10.8 × 9.1 cm)
    The Art Institute of Chicago,
      Alfred Stieglitz Collection

51. *The Terminal*
    Camera Work, no. 36
      (October 1911)
    Photogravure
    4¹³⁄₁₆ × 6¼ in. (12.2 × 16.0 cm)
    The Minneapolis Institute of Arts,
      gift of Julia Marshall

52. *Early New York: "Spring Showers"*
    1900
    Chloride print
    4¹⁄₁₆ × 2¹⁄₁₆ in. (10.4 × 5.3 cm)
    The Museum of Modern Art, New
      York, gift of Georgia O'Keeffe,
      Alfred Stieglitz Collection

53. *Spring Showers, New York* *
Camera Work, no. 36
  (October 1911)
Photogravure
9 1/16 × 3 5/8 in. (23.0 × 9.2 cm)
The Minneapolis Institute of Arts,
  gift of Julia Marshall

54. *The Hand of Man*
1902
Chloride print
3 1/2 × 4 3/4 in. (8.9 × 12.0 cm)
The Art Institute of Chicago,
  Alfred Stieglitz Collection

55. *The Hand of Man*
Camera Work, no. 1 (January 1903)
Photogravure
6 3/16 × 8 7/16 in. (15.8 × 21.4 cm)
The Minneapolis Institute of Arts,
  gift of Julia Marshall

56. *The Steerage*
1907
Gelatin silver print
3 7/16 × 4 7/16 in. (8.8 × 11.3 cm)
The Art Institute of Chicago,
  Alfred Stieglitz Collection

57. *The Steerage* *
Camera Work, no. 36
  (October 1911)
Photogravure
7 3/4 × 6 3/16 in. (19.7 × 15.8 cm)
The Minneapolis Institute of Arts,
  gift of Julia Marshall

Paul Strand
American, 1890-1976

58. *Man in a Derby, New York*
1916
Platinum print
12 13/16 × 9 15/16 in. (32.6 × 25.3 cm)
The Philadelphia Museum of Art,
  gift of the Estate of Paul Strand

59. *Photograph—New York* *
Camera Work, no. 49/50
  (June 1917)
Photogravure
8 15/16 × 6 3/4 in. (22.8 × 17.1 cm)
The Minneapolis Institute of Arts,
  William Hood Dunwoody Fund

60. *Shadows*
1916
Platinum print
13 1/4 × 9 3/16 in. (33.7 × 23.3 cm)
The Art Institute of Chicago,
  Alfred Stieglitz Collection

61. *Photograph*
Camera Work, no. 49/50
  (June 1917)
Photogravure
9 9/16 × 6 5/8 in. (24.4 × 16.9 cm)
The Minneapolis Institute of Arts,
  William Hood Dunwoody Fund

Clarence H. White
American, 1871-1925

62. *Drops of Rain*
1903
Platinum print
7 5/8 × 6 1/16 in. (19.4 × 15.4 cm)
The Museum of Modern Art,
  New York, gift of
  Mrs. Mervyn Palmer

63. *Drops of Rain* *
Camera Work, no. 23 (July 1908)
Photogravure
7 5/8 × 6 1/8 in. (19.4 × 15.6 cm)
The Minneapolis Institute of Arts,
  gift of Julia Marshall

64. *Morning*
1905
Platinum print
9 1/2 × 7 1/2 in. (24.1 × 19.1 cm)
The Metropolitan Museum of Art,
  Alfred Stieglitz Collection

65. *Morning*
Camera Work, no. 23 (July 1908)
Photogravure
8 × 6 1/16 in. (20.3 × 15.5 cm)
The Minneapolis Institute of Arts,
  gift of Julia Marshall

American, 1871–1925 and
  1864–1946

66. *Torso*
1907
Platinum print
16 5/16 × 12 1/16 in. (41.4 × 30.2 cm)
The Museum of Modern Art,
  New York

67. *Torso*
Camera Work, no. 27 (July 1909)
Photogravure
8 3/8 × 6 3/8 in. (21.4 × 16.2 cm)
The Minneapolis Institute of Arts,
  gift of Julia Marshall

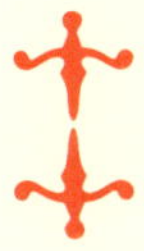

Exhibition Staff

Alan Shestack, *Director*
Timothy Fiske, *Associate Director*
Michael Conforti, *Chairman, Curatorial Division*
Carroll T. Hartwell, *Curator of Photography*
Christian A. Peterson, *Assistant Curator of Photography*
Anne Knauff, *Assistant Designer*
Elisabeth Sövik, *Associate Editor*
Mary Mancuso, *Exhibitions Coordinator*
Heidi Freerks, *Public Relations Assistant*
Gary Mortensen, *Photographer*
Robert Fogt, *Darkroom Technician*
Marilyn Bjorklund, *Registrar*
Karen Duncan, *Associate Registrar*
Claire Ouellette, *Assistant Registrar*
Roxy Ballard, John Black, Nina Chenault, Dennis Grodahl, Tom Jance, Doug Kroeger, Theo Manzavrakos, Esther Nelson, Patti Landres, *Works of Art Crew*
Suzanne Anderson, *Matting Technician*
R. Patrick Atherton, *Typographer*
Gordon Cable, *Chief of Security*

Six hundred copies of this catalogue were printed by Northstar Printing, Inc., Minneapolis.